CW00523946

BACK ON TOP!

BACK ON
TOP!

THE ALABAMA CRIMSON TIDE'S
2015-16 CHAMPIONSHIP
FOOTBALL SEASON

MARK MAYFIELD

Photography by Layton Dudley

SPORTS
PUBLISHING

Visit our website at www.sportspubbooks.com.

10 9 8 7 6 5 4 3 2 1

Library of Congress Cataloging-in-Publication Data is available on file.

Cover design by Tom Lau
Cover photo credit: AP Photo/Chris Carlson

Print ISBN: 978-1-61321-970-6
Ebook ISBN: 978-1-61321-981-2

Printed in the United States of America

Contents

Introduction—A Season to Remember   *1*

1. The Opener in Texas—Alabama vs. Wisconsin   7

2. Respecting the Opponent—Alabama vs. Middle
   Tennessee State   13

3. Disaster at Bryant-Denny—Alabama vs. Ole Miss   19

4. Coming Together—Alabama vs. Louisiana-Monroe   25

5. A Turning Point in the Rain—Alabama vs. Georgia   29

6. Homecoming—Alabama vs. Arkansas   39

7. Dominance in College Station—Alabama vs.
   Texas A&M   45

8. Fighting Through Fatigue—Alabama vs. Tennessee   49

9. Running Away with It—Alabama vs. LSU   55

10. Silencing the Cowbells—Alabama vs. Mississippi State 63

11. A Tin Horn—Alabama vs. Charleston Southern   69

12. Taking Care of Business—The Iron Bowl/Alabama vs.
    Auburn   75

13. The SEC Championship—Alabama vs. Florida   83

14. The Road to New York—Derrick Henry Wins the Heisman   91

15. Back to Work—Playoff Semifinal/Alabama vs. Michigan State   101

16. Champions Again—A Game for the Ages/Alabama vs. Clemson   109

17. A Decade of Excellence—Nick Saban's Alabama Legacy   121

18. Looking Ahead: 2016   135

Postscript   *141*

Alabama 2015 Roster   *155*

Alabama 2015 Season—By the Numbers   *161*

Author's Note and Acknowledgments   *189*

Resources   *195*

INTRODUCTION
A Season to Remember

THE CROWD DINING ON CHICKEN and roast beef in the Paul Bryant Conference Center thundered its applause as Nick Saban walked to the podium. It was October 9, 2015, one of those busy fall Fridays in Tuscaloosa. Outside, the campus buzzed with anticipation of the big homecoming football clash with Arkansas the next day.

Saban began his remarks by welcoming these hundreds of *Nick at Noon* luncheon attendees to homecoming weekend and, as always, thanked them for their support. Yet, clearly something else was on his mind, something that apparently had been bothering him for six days now, and he couldn't let it go.

Anyone who knows anything about Saban understands the man is a perfectionist on and off a football field, but it is in moments like this, during these kinds of speeches that have become routine for him, that he offers a public glimpse into a legendary obsession with every detail and every aspect of Alabama's program.

This was, after all, a day to talk about the next opponent, the big, bruising Razorbacks, who were coming to town bent on finally taking down an Alabama team for the first time since Saban's arrival as the Crimson Tide's coach in 2007. But first, the coach chose to make a point about last week's game with the Georgia Bulldogs over in Athens.

Specifically, Saban wanted to talk about the last few seconds of the third quarter against Georgia, a proud team that had the unenviable distinction of being the first opponent in six years to open as a favorite against Alabama. Not that it mattered. The Crimson Tide ultimately would win by 28 points in a driving rainstorm.

Saban, however, wasn't concerned with the scoreboard. He was focused on those waning seconds of the third quarter, or, more exactly, the ten seconds it took Georgia's star running back Nick Chubb to sprint through a gap and race 83 yards for a touchdown, untouched. Chubb's run did little more than cut Alabama's 38-3 lead to 38-10. It meant nothing in the final outcome and couldn't erase the humiliation dealt the Bulldogs in their own stadium.

Nevertheless, for Alabama, a defensive-minded team that had shut down Chubb the entire game up to that point, the lapse was egregious, simply not acceptable in a game the Crimson Tide owned from the second quarter. And for their coach, the man responsible for this unflinching domination, it was a cut to the heart.

"The key word here is focus," Saban said, slowly building his nearly week-old case. "If you don't have mental intensity in preparation, and every play in the game and in every game you play throughout the season, it's amazing how things can go from good to bad very quickly.

"This is one of the biggest challenges we have with young players. The players that we coach in college," he continued. "It's the culture of young people that we're trying to deal with, to get them to focus all the time. There was a great example in the game last week. We had stopped their run."

Saban looked out over the crowd, as if measuring their X's and O's football knowledge, and pressed on.

"Chubb had like 35 yards in rushing, or whatever, and (then came) one play, which we defended at least five times correctly in the game, which was just a zone dive play," Saban said. "Backer's got the A gap, safety's gonna come down and take the B gap. . . . And the safety comes down to the B gap, and the linebacker jumps over to the B gap. So we got two guys in the B gap and nobody in the A gap, and the ball spits and it spits so fast that the rest of the secondary could not converge on it. So one play, one player, lack of focus in terms of what he was supposed to do, and you go from a dominating defensive performance to an 83-yard touchdown and nobody touched the guy."

Focus.

It was not just a word heard by this audience paying a relatively modest $60 a plate at one of Saban's weekly fall luncheons. It was at the core of every drill, every workout, every practice, every meeting going forward during the 2015 season.

Ultimately, it would be the reason Saban and his team would dispatch Arkansas for the ninth consecutive time the next day, and three months later win a 45-40 thriller for the ages against Clemson in Glendale, Arizona, to claim Alabama's fourth national championship in seven years.

Saban would say repeatedly, both before and after the championship game, that this team was special, that it earned its way back to the top of college football by choosing to refocus and recommit after a shocking early-season home loss to Ole Miss. That had been a sloppy, turnover-filled game that led many national analysts to question whether Alabama's dynasty was over. Saban would use it as motivation, famously asserting that the media "had us dead and buried and gone. Gone."

En route to the championship, Alabama reeled off 12 consecutive victories following the Ole Miss game, including a 29-15 Southeastern Conference championship win over Florida, a 38-0 rout over Michigan State in the Cotton Bowl—which served as a College Football Playoff semifinal at AT&T Stadium in Arlington, Texas—and the victory over Clemson after a dramatic and wild back-and-forth clash at University of Phoenix Stadium. The fact that Alabama was able to secure the Clemson win following a gutsy—and successful—onside kick with the score tied, 24-24, in the fourth quarter underscored a simple fact: no program and coach could win four national titles in seven years without being prepared to step out of their comfort zone and do the unexpected with a game on the line.

For Alabama, that meant trying to dull the momentum of Clemson's outstanding quarterback, Deshaun Watson, by keeping the ball away from him. The surprise onside kick, called after Clemson lined up in a receiving formation that left a gap open on one side, was executed to perfection by Alabama's Adam Griffith, who popped the ball up toward the sideline. The Tide's Marlon Humphrey caught it over his shoulder near midfield, and Alabama not only maintained possession, but dramatically changed the game. Two plays later, Bama quarterback Jake Coker threw a 51-yard touchdown strike to a wide-open O.J. Howard, and the Crimson Tide took a 31-24 lead that it would never relinquish.

"We were tired on defense and weren't doing a great job of getting them stopped, and I felt like if we didn't do something or take a chance to change the momentum of the game that we wouldn't have a chance to win," Saban said.

Almost as unexpected as the onside kick was the emergence of a new star in the game: Howard. A big tight end at 6-foot-6 and 242 pounds, Howard possessed deceptive speed but had seldom been used on downfield throws. In fact, he caught his first touchdown pass of the season in the national championship game, a 53-yarder from Coker, followed by the 51-yard TD after that onside kick. Overall, he scorched Clemson for 208 yards receiving. His play, which earned him the Offensive Player of the Game trophy, overshadowed another impressive performance from Derrick Henry, the supersized running back who shattered the SEC rushing record with 2,219 yards and 28 touchdowns en route to the program's second-ever Heisman Trophy. Henry finished his college career with 158 yards and three touchdowns in the title game, his tenth 100-plus-yard game of the season.

Still, for all the four- and-five-star recruiting talent on Alabama's roster, for all the depth that most teams could never build, and for all the coaching talent on the sideline, the 2015 championship season came down to a team that reacted to adversity by pulling together instead of falling apart, and sacrificing their own egos during a magical run.

On January 12, 2016, a day after winning the championship, Saban reflected on the unity of his team.

"I didn't see one guy in the locker room after the game who was celebrating anything but a team win," he said. "I didn't see one guy pouting about 'I didn't get the ball enough.' I didn't see one guy pouting about 'how many yards I gained.' I didn't see one guy pouting about 'how much I got to play.' I didn't see that. I saw a bunch of happy guys based on what they were able to accomplish together as a group. . . . I think all the players are happy and proud for what the team was able to achieve and how they contributed to it over a long period of time; not just one game, 15 games."

It had started in Dallas. This long grind to a national championship.

CHAPTER ONE
The Opener in Texas

Alabama 35, Wisconsin 17

September 5, 2015

AT&T Stadium/Arlington, Texas

THE DYNASTY. WAS IT OVER?

Alabama entered the 2015 college football season ranked No. 3 in preseason polls, and for any other team that would have been a lofty start. After all, this was a team that for the second consecutive year would be breaking in a new quarterback and had lost key players to the NFL—among them the nation's top receiver (Amari Cooper) and the team's leading tackler (safety Landon Collins).

Add to that the fact the Crimson Tide began 2015 with a devastating New Year's Day loss in the Sugar Bowl to Ohio State in the semifinal round of the first-ever College Football Playoff, and analysts could be excused for dampening expectations.

Even so, this was Alabama, which had won three national championships in the previous six seasons. Crimson Tide fans, at least, expected no less than a return to the playoffs.

If this team was to meet those expectations, it would have to first win at a place that would later host one of this season's CFB Playoff semifinals: AT&T Stadium in Arlington, Texas. Home to the Dallas Cowboys. It was, however, familiar turf to Alabama. The Crimson Tide had opened its 2012 season here, defeating Michigan, 41-14, en route to a national championship season that ended with a blowout of Notre Dame in the Bowl Championship Series title game.

This time, the opponent would be another Big 10 power, Wisconsin, a team aiming to win a second consecutive game against a Southeastern Conference opponent. Back on New Year's Day, the Badgers had defeated Auburn, 34-31, in overtime of the Outback Bowl.

But these were not the same teams: Wisconsin, like Alabama, had lost key players to graduation and the NFL, including All-American running back Melvin Gordon, the 2014 Heisman Trophy runner-up. The Badgers also had a new coach, Paul Chryst, with a big challenge on his hands in his first game.

If Chryst and Wisconsin were feeling the pressure, the intensity was ramped up, as well, for Alabama. While the Badgers returned a veteran quarterback, Joel Stave, making his 29th start, Alabama had not yet named a starter to replace the departed Blake Sims. Nick Saban had quietly decided that two quarterbacks, Jake Coker and Cooper Bateman, would share playing time. Coker, however, would get this start.

"I made the decision on Thursday, not that it matters, to play both guys in the game," Saban disclosed later. "I told both guys we're not naming a starter. We're naming who's going to start in the game.

'Both of you guys have done extremely well throughout the course of fall camp. Both deserve an opportunity to play in the game.'"

On an opening Saturday that featured few major matchups nationally, the Alabama-Wisconsin game was a marquee game, and both teams would benefit from having started with tough opponents.

For Alabama's Derrick Henry, who had patiently waited his turn to become the Crimson Tide's featured back, the game would be an important national stage for a potential Heisman run, though he was listed nowhere among the favorites when the two teams kicked off on the field beneath AT&T Stadium's iconic, massive high-definition video screen.

Henry, at 6-foot-3, 242 pounds, wasted little time in making his presence known. Facing fourth-and-1 at Wisconsin's 37-yard line with 6:01 left in the first quarter, he took a handoff from Coker, burst through the line, and ran untouched to the end zone, exhibiting the kind of speed for such a large running back that would later propel him to the Heisman Trophy. But on this night it was simply a signal to opposing defenses: Henry would be a challenge to stop, especially if given a running start.

The touchdown gave Alabama a 7-0 lead, and the Crimson Tide would never trail. Henry finished with 147 yards on just 13 carries, and three touchdowns, in a dominant 35-17 victory. Alabama's defense did its part, as well, holding the Badgers to just 40 yards rushing.

"I think he's a fabulous player," Saban said, referring to Henry after the game. "He usually plays better as the game goes on, in terms of a workhorse-type guy. It was good to see him make some good runs out there. We think the guy can be a fantastic player for us."

Henry's performance was not a surprise—he had led the team in rushing during the 2014 season with 990 yards and 11 touch-downs, while sharing carries with starter T.J. Yeldon. But much of the attention before, during, and after this 2015 opener against Wisconsin focused on the two Crimson Tide quarterbacks competing for the starting job.

Coker, a Florida State transfer and fifth-year senior, who had first lost a quarterback competition with FSU's Jameis Winston and then with Alabama's Blake Sims, finally got his chance to lead an offense. He made the most of it, completing 15 of 21 passes for 213 yards and a touchdown. And more important, he made no major mistakes.

"I thought he did a nice job," Saban said. "I thought he was accurate with the ball. He didn't make any poor decisions. He didn't put the ball into coverage anywhere. He did a nice job of executing what we wanted him to do. So it created balance for us in our offense, and that was really good."

As if to defend even Coker's incompletions, Saban noted that most of them were "long balls that we had a chance on."

The Tide's other quarterback, Cooper Bateman, a redshirt sophomore from Salt Lake City, Utah, entered the game in the second half, going 7-for-8 passing with 51 yards and no touchdowns.

"Cooper got an opportunity and I thought he did fine, as well," Saban said.

Coker and Bateman spread the ball around judiciously, taking what the defense gave them. Alabama wide receiver Robert Foster led all receivers with four receptions for 50 yards, followed by running back Kenyan Drake's two catches for 48 yards, and ArDarius Stewart with four catches for 44 yards. Other receivers, including Richard Mullaney, a transfer from Oregon State, tight end O.J. Howard, and freshman Calvin Ridley, also contributed. The receiving-by-committee approach was interesting because, as events would later show, it would be Ridley who would emerge as the team's star receiver, and Howard who would ultimately grab the spotlight in the national championship game months later.

"We think O.J. Howard's a really good player who can make plays down the field," Saban said. "He's a mismatch guy. We probably need to do a little better job of getting him the ball more. And I think we will. He's had a great camp."

Overall, Alabama finished with 502 total yards to just 268 for the Badgers, most of Wisconsin's coming from Joel Stave's 228-yard, two-touchdown passing performance. Stave and his team continued to battle until Alabama safety Eddie Johnson picked off a pass with a minute left in the game and returned it 41 yards, effectively ending the game.

Substituting regularly during the second half, Saban said he was "not particularly pleased" with his second- and-third-team players' performances.

"We wanted to play a lot of players," he said. "They left their good players in, and I didn't think our guys played with the kind of poise and competitive character that is our standard and our expectation. But they'll certainly learn from that and will get better and improve."

Despite whatever problems Alabama's backups faced in the game, one thing was clear: this was just the beginning for what would become a stifling Alabama defense with stars like A'Shawn Robinson, Reggie Ragland, Jarran Reed, Jonathan Allen, Denzel Devall, Tim Williams, Cyrus Jones, Eddie Jackson, and freshman sensation Minkah Fitzpatrick, among others.

"We kind of dominated the line of scrimmage," Saban said. "We were able to stop their run. I thought we played real well defensively. Didn't get the turnovers like we wanted. Didn't always get off the field, like on third down like we wanted, but the guys really competed, and played hard."

Said Wisconsin coach Paul Chryst: "Certainly, hat's off to a very talented and well-coached Alabama team. They made more plays and were the better team tonight."

No sooner had the game ended than reporters were asking Saban if Coker would get the start the following week in the Tide's home opener against Middle Tennessee State.

"We don't have a plan yet," he said. "We have a 24-hour rule. We just won a big game against a good team. And I'm really proud of the way our guys came here and competed in the game."

CHAPTER TWO

Respecting the Opponent

Alabama 37, Middle Tennessee State 10

September 12, 2015

Bryant-Denny Stadium/Tuscaloosa

ALABAMA, NOW RANKED NO. 2 in the *Associated Press* and Coaches polls, returned home from the season opener against Wisconsin to a far less anticipated contest with Conference USA's Middle Tennessee State. This was one of those weeks that was ripe for a classic lecture from coach Nick Saban to reporters about respecting the opponent and playing to a high standard, no matter the competition.

The stage was set: Alabama was a 36-point favorite against the Blue Raiders, which had destroyed a Division 1 opponent,

Jackson State, 70-14, the previous week. It didn't take long for the Crimson Tide coach, and the media who regularly cover the team, to deliver one of the more entertaining news conferences of the season.

It was Monday, September 7, and here it was: a reporter seemed to suggest, with his question, that perhaps the Alabama coaches should use the opportunity against a lesser opponent to ramp up the in-game competition between Tide quarterbacks Jake Coker and Cooper Bateman.

Saban shot back.

"Everybody's got good football players and everybody needs to respect the opponent," Saban said, his voice and frustration level clearly rising. "I don't care if we're favored in a game or not favored in a game. The most important thing for our players is to focus on what they need to do to play their best. We took one step up on the climb, and we need to improve significantly. So we're approaching this game like it's the most important game of the season for us because it's the next game. And it's the next opportunity for us to try and get better.

"So we're not trying to create anything based on who we're playing, because we respect who we're playing, and I suggest everybody else does, too," he said. "I mean they just put 700 yards or something on a team, so we respect that. And we respect what they do. We respect their players and we respect their coaches. They go fast. It's probably going to be a hot day. We've got lots of issues and a lot of problems to deal with just in creating the kind of performance we want to create without creating something else."

Another question followed, but Saban couldn't get past the last one, still fuming.

"I'm sorry, you need to ask me that again," he said, his voice elevating. "I'm still on the last question because being able to concentrate on the right thing at the right time is critical to being successful. So what's the right thing at the right time now? Improving our team."

As the beginning of the game the following Saturday indicated, Saban's frustration was justified. The Crimson Tide's offense, behind Coker at quarterback, was lethargic in the first quarter. By the opening moments of the second quarter, Alabama held just a 7-3 lead, with two drives ending in punts, a failed fourth-down attempt, and a short touchdown drive made possible after a Middle Tennessee fumble. The Blue Raiders had nearly doubled Alabama's yardage in the first quarter, 120 to 66.

"We just weren't doing the little things right," Alabama tight end O.J. Howard said after the game. "It starts with paying attention to detail. Everything we did was our fault. Sometimes we may miss a block. It's things that we can fix, and that's the most important thing."

The fix started, actually, early in the second quarter. The Crimson Tide's offense began to take control, beginning with a 75-yard touchdown drive set up by a 42-yard sideline pass from Coker to Howard, and a 2-yard touchdown run by Derrick Henry.

Later in the same quarter, running back Kenyan Drake took a shovel pass from Coker, raced to the corner following a key block from Henry, and sprinted 69 yards to the MTSU 2-yard line. Henry took it in from there on the next play, and the Crimson Tide found some breathing room at 21-3. Minutes later, Alabama's Ronnie Harrison blocked a punt that bounced through MTSU's end zone and out of bounds for a safety, extending the lead to 23-3 at halftime.

Whatever the Crimson Tide's first-quarter woes against MTSU, they were nothing compared to what in-state rival Auburn faced at home 160 miles to the southeast in an shockingly-unexpected wire-to-wire battle with Football Championship Subdivision member Jacksonville State. The heavily favored Tigers had to score a late fourth-quarter touchdown to send the game into overtime and finally pulled out a 27-20 victory.

The close call at Auburn, ending just before kickoff of the Alabama-Middle Tennessee game, underscored Saban's point earlier in the week that no opponent should be taken lightly.

Soon after the second half started in Tuscaloosa, MTSU coughed up its third fumble of the game, this one by receiver Ed'Marques Batties, and Alabama began the half with great field position at the Blue Raiders' 29-yard line. The Middle Tennessee turnovers, four in all, including Cyrus Jones's second-quarter interception of a Brent Stockstill pass, were eerily similar to what would happen to Alabama a week later against Ole Miss.

But for now, early in the third quarter, Alabama turned to its second quarterback, Cooper Bateman, to lead the offense. The Crimson Tide, however, was unable to move the ball and even lost three yards. Making matters worse, placekicker Adam Griffith missed his second field goal of the game, this one from 49 yards. It was his fourth failed field goal attempt of the young season, and overall Alabama was not looking like it was ready for a return to the college football playoffs.

But there would be plenty of time to worry about that.

For now, Alabama made the most of its next possession, scoring on a 14-yard pass from Bateman to Drake, and then later in the third quarter mounting a crushing 11-play, 97-yard drive, capped by Henry's 28-yard touchdown run.

Leading, 37-3, midway through the fourth quarter, Bateman threw into double coverage downfield and paid for it: Middle Tennessee's Jeremy Cutrer picked it off and took it back 77 yards the other way, to Alabama's 20-yard line. Three plays later, the Blue Raiders scored on a 15-yard touchdown pass and salvaged some respect.

The final, at 37-10, was closer than expected by analysts, and the betting line at least, and left Alabama's players with plenty to correct as the team faced its first SEC game of the season against a talented Ole Miss team the following week.

Still, it was another productive performance from Alabama's offense, which gained 532 yards, and was led by Derrick Henry's 96 yards and three touchdowns rushing. Both Alabama quarterbacks had respectable, but uninspiring, performances: Coker went 15 of 26 passing for 214 yards, a touchdown, and an interception, while Bateman was 11-17 with a touchdown and the fourth-quarter interception that set up an MTSU score.

After the game, Saban was clearly not satisfied with the overall effort.

"These teams that are all good enough to expose you if you don't have the right focus and intensity on what you're doing to go out there and execute and do the job and finish," he said. "We obviously didn't do a great job of getting that point across. I don't think we finished like we need to. We didn't finish the game like we want to."

Overall, Saban concluded: "We really wanted to improve and play better this week than we played last week, and I'm not sure we accomplished that in all areas. There's some areas that we did improve, but there's many more things that we need to do a lot better."

Regardless, it was a win, and there seemed little time to look back with Ole Miss on the horizon. The Crimson Tide had lost to the Rebels, 23-17, in Oxford in 2014. This time the meeting would be in Tuscaloosa, and the winner would take a step up in the all-important SEC West race.

Alabama center Ryan Kelly said revenge wasn't a factor.

"They have a different team. We have a different team," he said but added: "You don't forget. I remember every single loss we ever had here."

As an offense, he said: "We want to keep our defense off the field, just because they (Ole Miss) go so fast. Putting together long drives like that is huge for this offense."

CHAPTER THREE
Disaster at Bryant-Denny

Ole Miss 43, Alabama 37

September 19, 2015

Bryant-Denny Stadium/Tuscaloosa

ONLY ONE TEAM—LSU—HAD BEEN ABLE to defeat Alabama in two consecutive years during Nick Saban's nine seasons in Tuscaloosa, and there was no compelling reason to believe that Ole Miss would be able to accomplish the same rare feat.

It was surprising enough that Alabama, which owns a lopsided record against Ole Miss, had lost to the Rebels a year earlier in Oxford. But this was Bryant-Denny Stadium, where Ole Miss had not defeated Alabama since 1988. The No. 2-ranked

Crimson Tide would be playing before a raucous home crowd of 101,821.

To be sure, the Rebels, with one of the SEC's best quarterbacks in Chad Kelly and a fast-paced offense that could test Alabama's outstanding front seven on defense, were legitimate contenders in the SEC West. The fact they had scored 76 and 73 points, respectively, in each of their first two games, albeit against far lesser, non-conference competition, did not go unnoticed by Alabama coaches, players, and their fans.

This would be a battle of two of the conference's best teams, with major national implications. It was a good early test for both teams, and the winner would control their own destiny in the SEC, while the loser would need help from other teams down the road if they were to rebound and make it to the conference championship game in Atlanta.

Seconds after the opening kickoff, it became obvious that only one of the teams (Ole Miss) was ready to handle the enormous pressure of the moment. Alabama, as it would turn out, could not stop making mistakes. It turned the ball over five times before the night was over.

The Crimson Tide's ArDarius Stewart, a talented and almost always reliable wide receiver, made the first mistake, fumbling the opening kickoff and giving Ole Miss possession at Alabama's 17-yard line. The Rebels, working against a stout and fast defense, could not take full advantage, moving the ball just two yards in three plays before settling for a 32-yard field goal and the game's first score less than a minute into the first quarter.

When Alabama's offense finally got to run a play from scrimmage on the next possession, it was Cooper Bateman who started at quarterback in place of Jake Coker, the starter in the Tide's first two games.

"We had some things in the game plan early that the quarterback was going to pull the ball on and do some things, so we thought that Cooper's speed would be a change of pace for them,"

Nick Saban said after the game, explaining the decision. "We thought that it could be a little bit of an element of surprise. We knew we were going to play Jake (Coker) in the game. Jake knew he was going to play in the game."

For a while at least, it seemed like the coaches had made the right decision. On the second play from scrimmage, Bateman's 30-yard pass to tight end O.J. Howard set Alabama up with a first down on the Rebels' 43-yard line. But four plays later, the Tide turned the ball over on downs to Ole Miss at the 34-yard line. Both teams exchanged punts, and the first quarter ended with Ole Miss still up, 3-0.

Alabama was able to tie it at 3-3 early in the second quarter with a 20-yard field goal from Adam Griffith, his first of the season after going 0-4 in the earlier games.

If it seemed that this was setting up to be a defensive battle early, Cooper Bateman changed the storyline with a deep throw that was intercepted and returned by Ole Miss's Trae Elston 28 yards to the Alabama 26. Once again, the Rebels had a short field, and this time they made the most of it. Led by Kelly and running back Jordan Wilkins, Ole Miss scored the game's first touchdown following a six-play, 26-yard drive.

Now up, 10-3, midway through the second quarter, Ole Miss was about to get yet another gift on the subsequent kickoff: Alabama running back Kenyan Drake fumbled at the Crimson Tide 19-yard line, and the Rebels' Carlos Davis recovered it at the 18.

Already benefitting from turnovers that had given them field position at Alabama's 17- and 26-yard lines, Ole Miss now had another short-field opportunity. A pass interference call against Alabama moved the ball to the Tide 4-yard line. It took three plays, but the Rebels scored when Chad Kelly tucked the ball and ran it in from the 4 on third down.

With a successful extra point kick, Ole Miss led, 17-3, before a stunned crowd at Bryant-Denny. This was not going well for the home team. Alabama fans had seen some rare losses in Saban's nine seasons but never saw the team imploding like this.

On Alabama's next series, Jake Coker entered the game for the first time and led a 15-play, 75-yard drive that ended with a 9-yard touchdown pass to Richard Mullaney. Along the way, Coker had rushed for 15 yards of his own and began establishing a reputation for toughness that would stick with him for the rest of the season.

Ole Miss led, 17-10, at halftime, but Alabama had more than doubled the Rebels in yardage, 214-95. Nevertheless, turnovers were, and would remain, the big difference in this game.

Yet it wouldn't simply be the Crimson Tide's mistakes that shocked the home crowd and a national television audience. On Ole Miss's first drive of the second half, quarterback Kelly bobbled a high snap and under pressure from Alabama defenders lobbed a desperation pass that was deflected by the Rebels' LaQuon Treadwell, then miraculously caught by wide receiver Quincy Adeboyejo, who ran it in for a 66-yard touchdown. The turnovers had been bad enough for Alabama. Now a fluke touchdown had added to the misery.

The Rebels later tacked on two field goals and led, 30-10, until Alabama finally answered with a nine-play, 69-yard touchdown drive late in the third quarter, led by a 31-yard run by Derrick Henry and Coker's 3-yard keeper for the touchdown.

Trailing, 30-17, early in the fourth quarter, Alabama cut the deficit to 30-24 with an 8-yard touchdown pass from Coker to ArDarius Stewart. But the Rebels answered quickly, taking advantage of blown coverage in Alabama's secondary with a 73-yard touchdown throw from Kelly to Cody Core. A failed 2-point conversation left the score at 36-24 with nearly 12 minutes left in the game.

On Alabama's next series, yet another turnover—a Coker interception—again gave the Rebels a short field, this time at the

Tide's 31-yard line. Ole Miss scored three plays later on a 24-yard pass from Kelly to Treadwell. The lead, now at 43-24, seemed insurmountable. But Alabama was not yet done.

Coker led the offense on a 14-play, 75-yard drive, capped by Henry's 2-yard touchdown run. Down, 43-30, the Tide successfully recovered an onside kick, then drove 30 yards for another touchdown, this one ending with a 2-yard pass from Coker to Mullaney in the end zone. An extra point left the Tide just six points down at 43-37. There was hope, and Bryant-Denny was rocking again.

After forcing an Ole Miss punt, Alabama had the ball, backed up at its own 7-yard line, but with a chance to complete the comeback with 3:01 left in the game. On the first play, Coker kept the ball for a 26-yard gain, and plenty of time left to run the offense. On the next play, however, Coker threw deep, and the ball was intercepted at the Ole Miss 32-yard line. Alabama's defense held the Rebels again, and the Tide got the ball back one last time with just 31 seconds left and no timeouts. But there would be no miraculous finish. Four consecutive incomplete passes ended the game.

Afterward, Saban seemed to take a big-picture view of the loss, noting the team's strong character, even in defeat.

"The key thing for our players now is how you're going to respond to a loss," Saban said. "I really was proud of the way our players fought back in the game, to get the game 30 to 24, then we gave up a big play. Then we got down by 20 points, and we fought back again and actually had the ball with an opportunity maybe to have a chance to win the game. I really like the resilience of our players. They played for 60 minutes. They fought back, but the mistakes that we made, all that we gave away, we could not overcome."

Rebels coach Hugh Freeze seemed as joyful as his team but also understood that it was a long season, and just one game.

"Oh man, what a game," he said. "It was definitely a four-quarter battle. We thought we had it put away a couple of times, and they just wouldn't go away. That's a credit to their staff and the character of their team and their kids. The great thing about it is we can improve so much from this. There are so many things we could've done better tonight. You know, they had a hundred plays and that just about wore our defense out."

To be sure, Alabama's offense, despite the turnovers, had managed to move the football on an Ole Miss defense led by the much-heralded Nkemdiche brothers, Denzel and Robert, who combined for 16 tackles. The Crimson Tide racked up 502 total yards, including 127 yards rushing from Derrick Henry, and 288 yards passing combined from Coker and Bateman.

Ole Miss finished with 433 yards, including 341 yards passing from Chad Kelly, and it proved to be enough.

"This is awesome," Kelly said. "This is what you dream about."

For Alabama, the loss would turn into the kind of motivation that would eventually lead to a championship, though no one could have known it for sure at the time. The Tide also lost starting wide receiver Robert Foster for the season, out with a torn rotator cuff. But there was even opportunity in that. Already, freshman Calvin Ridley had emerged as a great new talent, sharing receiving duties with Foster on the field opposite ArDarius Stewart. Now Ridley would be called on as a starter, and he would more than live up to the challenge.

It was a crushing loss, but there was plenty of football still to be played.

"You guys have no idea how bad this hurts, but we are going to get back at it," said Alabama defensive end Jonathan Allen. "The same thing happened last year and we ended up going to the playoffs. We're going to get another chance, and get another time to prove ourselves, so we can't do anything now other than move on to the next team."

Said O.J. Howard: "I like the fight in our team, and it showed a lot about who we are, and what we can do going forward."

CHAPTER FOUR

Coming Together

Alabama 34, Louisiana-Monroe 0

September 26, 2015

Bryant-Denny Stadium/Tuscaloosa

FACED WITH THE LOSS TO Ole Miss, and ensuing questions nationally about whether Alabama was still among college football's dominant programs, the Crimson Tide's veteran players took action. They quietly called a team meeting to remind one another, and the younger players in particular, that their goals were still in front of them—that they and their coaches, not the critics, determined their fate.

"We realized it was time to bring everybody together and just kind of re-state what we want from this team this year," cornerback Cyrus Jones told reporters when the news of the meeting surfaced a week later. "We can't dwell on what happened in the Ole Miss game. That's gone. That's in the past. We have to focus on the future."

The tone of the meeting, according to players who described it later, centered on a commitment to ignore distractions, stay together as a team, and focus on finishing.

"At the end of the day it's (about) all the guys in that room," said center Ryan Kelly. "We're the guys that go out there every day (at) practice, bleed together, sweat together. Nobody else is really doing that besides us. So at the end of the day, it doesn't matter about anybody else's opinion about what we do. It's about who's in that room, who's on that field."

The meeting notwithstanding, Alabama still had to go out and get it done on the field. A year earlier, Alabama had lost to Ole Miss but managed to run the table the rest of the way, win the SEC championship, and make it to the playoff semifinals. Could the Tide do it again? One thing was almost certain: there could be no more losses.

If Alabama, which had dropped to No. 12 in the rankings, were to climb back up the ladder, it would have to start this week against Louisiana-Monroe. This was a program indelibly familiar to Alabama fans. The Warhawks had come into Bryant-Denny Stadium as 24-point underdogs in 2007, Saban's first year in Tuscaloosa, and upset the Crimson Tide, 21-14. It was a humiliating defeat for a proud program bent on making it back to the nation's elite.

This year the Warhawks were even larger underdogs, but there would be no upset. This was not 2007, and this was not the same Alabama team. It was, however, a team with something to prove after losing to Ole Miss. Even in the loss, Alabama had found its starting quarterback in Jake Coker. Against Louisiana-Monroe he had an adequate, but far from spectacular, day, completing 17 of 31 passes for 158 yards, three touchdowns, and one interception. His receivers, who dropped four balls in the first half, didn't make his day any easier. Both Coker and his offense improved in the second half, finishing with 303 total yards, but far under the 512-yard average they had coming into the game.

Alabama's defense, by contrast, had its best game yet, shutting out Louisiana-Monroe en route to a 34-0 Alabama victory. Led by a smothering defensive front seven, the Crimson Tide held the Warhawks to just 92 total yards, including nine rushing. Alabama also recorded six quarterback sacks, and defensive backs Geno Matias-Smith and Ronnie Harrison each had an interception. The monstrous defensive performance would lay the foundation for even more impressive feats to come against more talented competition.

"We played with a lot of toughness, especially on defense," Nick Saban said. "To give a team around 90 yards is really good. I thought we tackled well in space and we got a couple turnovers. We did a good job on third down, especially in the first half, and that was really positive."

Offensively, Saban said the team was still trying to find its identity but added: "We played it pretty tight to the vest today and I think we probably need to do a little more. I thought Jake (Coker) did a good job, and however you look at the stops, you've got to look at the drops. That wasn't really his fault. He made some good throws. There was probably a couple times that he wishes he would have done it a little different, in terms of going to somebody else, and those are the things we need to work out and get better at."

Coker, meeting with reporters after the game, said he thought he got better in the second half but added: "I've got a long way to go."

Although Derrick Henry had carried the ball 23 times for 127 yards and a touchdown against Ole Miss a week earlier, he was used far less against Louisiana-Monroe, carrying just 13 times for 52 yards and a touchdown. Saban explained that Henry "was sick part of the week. He practiced on Thursday, but I just didn't want to wear the guy out today. I wanted to give other guys the opportunity to play, and I thought they developed and did a good job."

Those other guys included Kenyan Drake, who ran ten times for 66 yards, and Damien Harris, with four carries for 23 yards. Drake, in particular, seemed to be making the best of his opportunity four games into the 2015 season, having missed most of the 2014 season after suffering a broken leg against Ole Miss in the third game of that year.

Another bright note for Alabama was placekicker Adam Griffith's two field goals—one from 40 yards and the other from 35. Griffith had missed each of his first four attempts of the season before making a 20-yard field goal against Ole Miss. Now, he had made three in a row.

"We have a lot of confidence in him that he is capable," Saban said. "I think he just has to think the right things and focus on the technique that he needs to use to have success, and when he does that he is a very good kicker."

From his perspective, Louisiana-Monroe head coach Todd Berry said Alabama "didn't do anything that surprised us. We just didn't do what we were asking them to do. I liked our game plan coming in, but we still didn't execute as well as we would have liked. Alabama's a good football team, and it should be a good game (Alabama versus Georgia) next week."

Three weeks earlier, the Warhawks had met Georgia in the season opener for both teams. Georgia won, 51-14, and they would open as a slight favorite against Alabama. It would be the first time Alabama had been an underdog, albeit by just a single point, in 73 games, dating back to the 2009 SEC championship game against Florida.

CHAPTER FIVE
A Turning Point in the Rain

Alabama 38, Georgia 10

October 3, 2015

Sanford Stadium/Athens

DOUBT WAS EVERYWHERE.

Alabama had delivered a 34-0 shutout in its last game and still dropped a spot, to No. 13, in the latest *Associated Press* and *USA Today*/Amway Coaches polls. Some analysts were simply questioning whether the Crimson Tide could get through a grueling schedule without another loss. Others seemed certain the program's time had come and gone.

The Ole Miss loss hung heavy.

"Welcome, everyone, to the fall of a champion," Matt Hayes of *Sporting News* wrote after that game. "There is no greater indicator of a lost dynasty, no more prominent red flag, than ignoring the obvious: this is not the same Alabama program of years gone by."

Fox Sports's Clay Travis, known to stir it up, predicted that when Alabama, with its now "ordinary" defense, would "roll into Georgia and lose, it will be a perfect capstone to the rise and fall of the Tide dynasty."

Hayes and Travis were far from alone. *USA Today*'s Dan Wolken went on the *ESPN/SEC Network*'s *The Paul Finebaum Show* and said: "The dynasty argument is about a state of mind, a state of being. That's gone. That no longer exists at Alabama. They have no right to it anymore. They can still be very, very good. But they're going to have to improve. I don't think what happened Saturday was a fluke by any means. I picked Ole Miss."

To be fair, Alabama had not looked anything like the team that had won three national championships since Nick Saban arrived as coach. Not only had the Crimson Tide recently lost at home to Ole Miss, the program had also lost two consecutive Sugar Bowl games, first to Oklahoma on January 2, 2014, and then to Ohio State in the national playoff semifinal a year later.

"No one fears Alabama anymore," wrote *CBS Sports*'s Jon Solomon.

As if to underscore Solomon's point, Alabama opened as a 1-point underdog to Georgia, the first time in 73 games the Crimson Tide was not a favorite. With the game in Athens, and No. 8-ranked Georgia undefeated at 4-0, including a pair of SEC victories, the fact the game was a virtual pick-em in Las Vegas was understandable. But to Alabama players, it was simply more motivation.

What some national analysts failed to understand, perhaps, was that Alabama coaches and players were eager to get to Athens, with an opportunity to re-establish the kind of dominance the program thrived on. The Crimson Tide had been an excellent road team under Saban, and that didn't bode well for Georgia.

It had been in Athens, ironically, where Saban and his program had emerged back in 2008 as a national contender after jumping out to a 31-0 lead against the higher-ranked and favored Bulldogs, and cruising to a 41-30 win. That game, labeled a "blackout" because Georgia fans had been asked to wear all black to show their support, had been a humiliating defeat for the home team.

There was more humiliation to come, this time on the first Saturday of October in 2015.

Some, like Paul Finebaum, host of one of college football's most popular call-in talk shows on *ESPN Radio* and *The SEC Network*, saw the signs early that morning in Athens.

"I talked to a guy at the hotel, some Dawg fan, and I asked, 'What do you think?' He said, 'Man, we're not gonna win,'" Finebaum said. "It was as if all the bravado from Georgia fans for months evaporated that morning. I mean, it was like, 'Nick Saban is actually in town.' And from that moment on I really believed that Alabama was going to win the game."

Unlike 2008, there was no blackout awaiting the Crimson Tide in Georgia's sold-out Sanford Stadium. But there was a gauntlet of Georgia players who crowded a corner of the sideline and verbally jousted with Crimson Tide players as they rushed onto the field for pregame warm-ups. No punches were thrown, and what could have been a far more serious moment dissipated quickly. But the dust-up underscored the emotions running high for what would become a defining game for both teams.

Although the consensus among observers on both sides seemed to be that Georgia players started the taunting, Alabama coach Nick Saban took notice and didn't like what he saw from his own team. "I got really pissed," Saban said. "I said, 'All right, are we going to go through this again? We're gonna be emotional and not be able to execute and do what we're supposed to do?' That's not who we are. So we're focused on playing football and doing our job. And they settled down and did a good job of that."

Said Alabama cornerback Cyrus Jones: "We knew it was going to be a fired-up game. They were going to be ready to come out and play their best, and so were we. When the clock started, you saw what happened."

Indeed. Much of the college football world, watching on the *CBS Sports* broadcast, saw what happened as a steady rain turned into a torrential downpour inside the stadium. During a four-and-a-half-minute span of the second quarter, Alabama scored 21 points, took a 24-3 lead, kept a stranglehold on Georgia's much-heralded rushing offense, and finished with a crushing 38-10 victory over the Bulldogs.

The final score, much like the game back in 2008, didn't fully reflect the absolute domination Alabama held over Georgia throughout the contest. This was a beatdown, and afterward a clearly disappointed and subdued Mark Richt, Georgia's head coach, said as much: "I want to give credit to Alabama. They did a great job tonight. They certainly whipped us pretty good. We didn't have many counterpunches for them. We just got out-coached and out-played today."

By the end of the season, Richt would be forced to resign after 15 seasons at Georgia. It was widely assumed that such a devastating, high-profile home loss hastened his departure. Replacing him after the season would be a man on the opposite sideline that afternoon—Alabama defensive coordinator Kirby Smart.

The game in Athens proved that Alabama was back, not only with another signature win, but with the confidence and swagger it had maintained throughout the dynasty that so many analysts had claimed was over. Jake Coker had his best game and now was in full control of the offense. Derrick Henry, who scored the game's first touchdown with a 30-yard, rapid-fire burst up the middle in the second quarter, had just entered the Heisman Trophy race. Calvin Ridley, the sensational freshman receiver, caught five passes for 120 yards and a touchdown and emerged as the successor to the departed, great Amari Cooper. And Alabama's defensive front seven established themselves as a dominant force, stifling for most of the game two of the SEC's best running backs in Georgia's Nick Chubb and Sony Michel.

It was as complete an effort as any game in college football up until this point, with Alabama scoring in all three phases of the game—offense, defense, and special teams.

"I told them (the players) before the game that the plan that we had for them, ordinary men couldn't go out there and get it done," Saban said. "We needed them to be extraordinary, and they were, and they were special, and they've been that way all year. And I know they've been criticized a lot, but I thought we played an outstanding game today."

Adding to the enormity of the win was the fact that it had started quietly enough as rain descended on the stadium. It was almost as if Alabama were a sleeping giant in the first quarter. The Crimson Tide had even spotted Georgia great field position at the Alabama 42-yard line after a Henry fumble. But this was not going to be another Ole Miss game. Far from it. Alabama's defense forced a Georgia punt on that possession, and by the end of the first quarter the Tide held a 3-0 lead following a 29-yard Adam Griffith field goal.

Early in the second quarter, Georgia tied the game with a 27-yard field goal, but, as the Bulldogs' Mark Richt would later say, "the dam broke a little bit" minutes later. Or . . . more like a lot.

Derrick Henry took a handoff with fewer than nine minutes left in the second quarter and bolted untouched up the middle for a 30-yard touchdown. It was only the beginning of the disappointment for most of the 92,746 fans crammed into Sanford Stadium.

The next few minutes would tell the full tale: Alabama was about to put on a football clinic of offense, defense, and special teams that would leave Georgia reeling.

On their next possession, stalled and unable to get any traction against Alabama's defense, the Bulldogs prepared to punt from near their own goal line. When the ball was snapped, Alabama freshman defensive back Minkah Fitzpatrick rushed through untouched, blocked the punt, snapped it up on the 1-yard line without breaking stride, and scored the Crimson Tide's second touchdown in fewer than four minutes. An extra point expanded Alabama's lead to 17-3. It would quickly get worse for Georgia.

After the Tide defense forced another punt from deep in Georgia's own territory, the Alabama offense set up with a first down at the Bulldogs' 45-yard line. Jake Coker went deep on the first play, throwing a touchdown strike to an open Calvin Ridley racing behind Georgia's defensive backs. Another extra point and it was Alabama 24, Georgia 3.

Faced with an onslaught, the Bulldogs pulled their starting quarterback, Grayson Lambert, in favor of Brice Ramsey late in the first half, but it would make no difference. By halftime, Alabama had nearly doubled the Bulldogs in yardage and, per- haps more important, had held Georgia's standout running back, Nick Chubb, to just 39 yards on ten carries.

The second half would bring an even more furious rainstorm, and Alabama seemed to revel in it.

Just a minute and a half into the third quarter, Tide safety Eddie Jackson intercepted a Brice Ramsey pass and ran it back 50 yards for another Alabama touchdown. Thousands of Georgia fans began heading for the exits with the Crimson Tide up, 31-3, and no sign and no hope that the Bulldogs could do anything about it.

It only got worse for Georgia a few minutes later when Coker scored another Alabama touchdown, this one from two yards out to cap a four-play, 38-yard drive. Alabama now led, 38-3, with ten minutes left in the third quarter. This one was all but over.

Nevertheless, the Georgia fans who remained in the stadium finally got something to cheer about when Chubb, taking advantage of a blown Alabama defensive gap assignment, raced 83 yards for a touchdown as the final seconds ticked away in the third quarter. The score cut Alabama's lead to 38-10 and following a scoreless fourth quarter became the game's final score.

It had been a masterful, if not perfect, performance by the Crimson Tide. Henry finished the game with 26 carries for 146 yards and a touchdown. Ridley stood out with 120 receiving yards and his own TD.

"Calvin's played well for us all year long," Saban said. "He's obviously getting more opportunities now that Robert Foster is out. He shows a lot of maturity for a freshman in terms of the way he plays, and doesn't make a lot of mistakes. He made a really big play today, and has played well all year. I know he dropped one last week, but you kind of live and learn; he's a very confident guy who I think is very focused and really shows a lot of maturity for a freshman."

Jake Coker, exhibiting the kind of confidence that Saban and Alabama offensive coordinator Lane Kiffin had wanted to see all season, completed 11 of 16 passes for 190 yards and a touchdown.

"I think everybody settled in and just got comfortable, and we started playing like we can play," Coker said. "I've just got to keep studying what I need to study, do the right things, and we'll see what happens from there. I felt real good out there."

Saban, soaked like everyone else from the rain, expressed pride in his players.

"I thought this was a really difficult challenge for them," he said. "Every part of the game. There were tough conditions out there.

The quarterback did a fantastic job. We moved the ball effectively on offense. Made a couple of explosive plays. The defense did a great job except for the one long run. Got in the wrong gaps. But we scored on special teams, scored on defense, scored on offense. So we scored on all three areas of the game. I can't tell you how proud I am of the players, the coaches. People hung in there and really believe in this team. I believe in this team."

The game plan, Saban said, had been to mix what Alabama does best, running the football, with play-action passes. The idea, he said, was get a lead and keep it.

"We were going to play the game close to the vest and try to run the ball, throw play-action passes because we did not want to get behind in the game," Saban said. "We were fortunate to get ahead in the game with some good execution, made a couple of big plays, and blocked a punt. I think it's very difficult to come back and get taken out of your game plan in situations like that. Our guys did a great job of executing the plan."

The coach also had plenty to say about his defense, noting that Georgia "couldn't run the ball on us, except for the one long run," and kept the Bulldogs in third-and-long situations, an unenviable task, made all the worse by the hard rain.

"So I thought our defense front seven did a great job, but I thought we played well in the secondary, as well," Saban said.

Alabama players made it known, clearly, that part of their motivation had been to prove the naysayers wrong, although more than that, to stay together as a team and do their jobs.

"I think we made a big statement," said Cyrus Jones. "Obviously we had a tough loss to Ole Miss. Everybody was kind of counting us out. We just knew that we weren't out of it. We take pride in just dominating every phase of the game. We had a great week of practice and I think it showed up. Everybody was out there playing fast. Everybody knew what we had to do. The defense was on the same page and the offense made big plays, as well.

"Once we're on the same page, it's hard to stop us," he said.

The underdog role also made a difference.

"We don't think we're the underdog in any game we're playing," Jones said. "But at the same time, it's not about what outside people say. We know what type of team we have. We just wanted to come in here, make a statement, and dominate every phase of the game and I think we did that."

Said Alabama offensive tackle Cam Robinson: "Definitely, that's something we don't take too kind to, is being underdogs. We had a little more focus and a little more intensity just because of the underdog role."

In a statement that would foreshadow Derrick Henry's eventual run to the Heisman Trophy, Robinson issued what amounted to a warning to opposing defenses: "The more we wear them out during the game, you can tell on the field those guys don't want to tackle Derrick. He's a load coming downhill."

Overall, said Saban, Alabama took a major step forward. But as always, the coach saw plenty of things that still needed work as Alabama prepared to leave Athens, head back to Tuscaloosa, and get ready for a homecoming date with Arkansas.

"We improved. We're getting better," he said. "It's one game. I think we have to show that we can play with consistency. I don't think we finished the game like we need to, which is something we can learn from. If it was a closer game, that wouldn't have been a good thing. We didn't take the air out of it on offense (late in the game). We couldn't run the ball like we wanted to. We gave up a big play on defense, but it's one game."

But he was quick to add: "I thought they played their best game of the year today, obviously, against a very good team."

CHAPTER SIX
Homecoming

Alabama 27, Arkansas 14

October 10, 2015

Bryant-Denny Stadium/Tuscaloosa

FOR 14 FULL MINUTES, NICK Saban's news conference inside the University of Alabama's Mal M. Moore Athletic Facility on October 5, 2015, was routine. The coach, clad in a pink golf shirt, stood at a podium, recounted his team's impressive performance at Georgia, and pitched ahead to the upcoming Arkansas game.

"You really have to have your jaw set to play well against the type of things they (Arkansas) do," he said, his hands resting on the podium, where a Coca-Cola bottle, its label carefully turned toward the cameras, was prominently displayed. "And they have been a very efficient, effective passing team to go with a great running game. So this is going to be a real challenging game."

There was no indication that Saban's tone would change, or the news conference would go off the rails. But *YouTube* is filled with clips from Saban's news conferences like the exchange that was about to happen. For reporters who have been there in the line of fire, it's as if Saban picks his moments, waiting for the right time and the right question to get his message out. After all, for a man who meticulously runs every detail of his famed "process," news conferences are simply part of it. What may look like a knee-jerk reaction to some was anything but.

This time it came 14 minutes into a 16.5-minute news conference, and it began when a reporter asked the coach what he and his staff would say, particularly to young players, to minimize "noise" and distractions from sources outside the program.

Saban had his opening.

"Well, I say the same thing as when y'all buried us last week, alright, and all that, that it really doesn't matter what you think, and it really doesn't matter what you say, and I'm hoping that nobody on our team is playing for you," Saban said, his hands moving and his voice rising. "I hope they're playing for each other, and their team, and what they want to accomplish, and not what you think. Because that's not certainly what I'm doing. I'm coaching and working for our players and our team to be as good as it can be. And if that's not pleasing to somebody else, it's not pleasing to somebody else. I said before, I believe in our team. I do believe in our team, and we're gonna work hard to make our team better. And I hope the players respond the right way.

"And it's not gonna be for you," Saban thundered. "The fans, yes . . . cause if it was up to you, we're six feet under already. We're dead and buried and gone. Gone!"

It was over, or was it? Saban paused for a moment and added: "So if that was the case we'd have to get respirators out or something down there, alright, to put life back in people."

Sensing another question, Saban calmly cautioned: "Better make it good now, because I'm about half-fired up here."

The exchange with beat reporters lasted only a couple of minutes, but it had set the tone for the remainder of Alabama's season. This was a team playing with a chip on its shoulder. The rout at Georgia had sent a signal to college football: Alabama was still elite, and any opponent who didn't understand that did so at its own peril.

For all his perfectionism, Saban has always supported and defended his players, most notably in losses. He wasn't about to let the media define his team. The players and coaches would determine their own fate.

That didn't, however, make the task against Arkansas any easier.

True to form for a Bret Bielema-coached team, the Razorbacks came into Bryant-Denny Stadium the following Saturday determined to make Alabama earn every yard. Arkansas had lost to Alabama by only a point back in Fayetteville in 2014, and by all appearances they had the potential to be an even better team this time around, never mind that the Razorbacks had already lost three of their first five games.

This one was brutal from the beginning, and the Razorbacks took a 7-3 lead into halftime. The Crimson Tide had entered the Arkansas red zone twice with only a field goal to show for it. Worse, Jake Coker had been intercepted twice on deep throws in the first half, including one that, combined with an unsportsmanlike penalty, had set Arkansas up on Alabama's 12-yard line, leading to a Razorbacks touchdown.

The bright spot was Alabama's defense, which had overwhelmed Arkansas, holding the Razorbacks to just 77 total yards in the first half. Again, Alabama's own offense had far better numbers, with 204 yards, but little to show for it.

The momentum finally changed, and quickly, late in the third quarter when Coker hit a wide-open Calvin Ridley with an 81-yard touchdown throw. Alabama took a 10-7 lead into the fourth quarter.

"It was a great lift for the offense," said running back Derrick Henry. "I felt like somebody had to make a play for the offense, and he (Ridley) made a play."

Said Coker: "Calvin did his job, ran the right route, and he got the job done. Now that he's getting more and more comfortable, it's getting exciting to see what he can do."

Alabama added another touchdown (a 3-yard pass into the end zone from Coker to Richard Mullaney) early in the fourth quarter following a 43-yard drive and tacked on a field goal minutes later. Leading, 20-7, later in the quarter, Cyrus Jones's 27-yard punt return set up the Crimson Tide in the Razorbacks' red zone again at the 16-yard line. Three runs from Henry, including the final 1-yard for a touchdown, and Alabama led, 27-7, in the waning moments of the game. But Arkansas was not quite finished: the Razorbacks scored on a 54-yard touchdown pass with just 1:37 left in the game.

For Alabama, it was a hard-fought 27-14 win, and another step on the road back to an SEC championship and a shot at the playoffs. For now, the Crimson Tide improved its overall record to 5-1 (2-1 in the SEC). Offensively, Alabama managed nearly 400 yards against the Razorbacks, including 262 and two touchdowns from Coker through the air, along with two interceptions.

Defensively, Reggie Ragland led all Alabama defenders with eight tackles and a sack.

"We're communicating (on the field as a defense)," Ragland said. "We're having fun. We're moving around, playing hard, just all gelling together."

While Alabama had seemed to put on a clinic in the rain in Georgia a week earlier, this game was more of a hard grind, physically taxing, and a battle in the trenches.

"I was really pleased with the way we played in the second half," Saban said. "I thought we didn't play poorly in the first half, we just turned the ball over and didn't finish drives in the red zone. We also gave them the ball on the 8-yard line, which is where they got the touchdown. At halftime, in games like this, we knew this would be a tough game. We had a tough game with these guys last year, and we know what kind of team they are. They're well coached, and they play with a lot of toughness."

Said Arkansas coach Bret Bielema: "Unfortunately, it's a loss, but I know this: we're better in week six than we were in week one. We'll take a bye week and use the time to get some guys healthy overall, and come back with six games left to determine what our future is. As a football team, I think they'll bounce back and respond as they always have, and we'll see where they can go."

His words were prophetic: Arkansas would go on to win five of its last six games, including a wild 53-52 overtime upset of Ole Miss that would open the door for Alabama to retake the lead and control its own destiny in the SEC West race.

CHAPTER SEVEN

Dominance in College Station

Alabama 41, Texas A&M 23

October 17, 2015

Kyle Field/College Station

EXPECTATIONS WERE SOARING FOR UNDEFEATED and ninth-ranked Texas A&M, as 105,733 fans took their seats at Kyle Field in College Station for a showdown with Alabama. Ranked No. 10, the Crimson Tide had just survived a punishing battle with Arkansas, while the Aggies had the luxury of a bye week to prepare for this pivotal SEC West game.

For the second time this season, Alabama would have to beat a top 10 team on the road if it had any chance of repeating as SEC champions, and perhaps making a return trip to the playoffs.

Texas A&M's 5-0 record was no fluke: the Aggies had defeated two SEC West powers, Arkansas and Mississippi State, and dominated a good Arizona State team, 38-17, in the season opener.

It would take another complete performance from Alabama in all phases of the game to win this one in front of a hostile crowd in one of college football's greatest environments. Could the Crimson Tide deliver? It would take only midway through the first quarter before there was an answer.

Alabama's Minkah Fitzpatrick intercepted Aggies quarterback Kyle Allen's pass out in the flat and raced 33 yards down the sideline for a touchdown with 7:53 left in the first quarter. It would be the first of four interceptions, including three returned for touchdowns, by Alabama defenders during the game. They included another 55-yard interception and touchdown return from Fitzpatrick in the fourth quarter. He would become the first Alabama player in history with two pick-six plays in one game. Safety Eddie Jackson added his own spectacular 93-yard interception return for a touchdown in the second quarter en route to the Tide's 41-23 rout of the Aggies.

For their efforts, Fitzpatrick and Jackson jointly were named National Defensive Players of the Week by the Football Writers Association of America.

While Alabama's defense was scoring seemingly at will against a flustered Kyle Allen, the Crimson Tide's big running back, Derrick Henry, was punishing the Aggies on offense. He ran over, around, and through Texas A&M's defense for a career-high 236 yards and two touchdowns, including a 55-yard bolt through the middle of the Aggies' defense in the first quarter.

Henry was a workhorse, carrying the ball 32 times for a 7.4-yard average.

"He's just so tough," quarterback Jake Coker said after the game. "He just never stops, and whether it's the beginning of the game or the end. It's the same way. He's just punishing people. The only time anybody gets a good shot on him is when he doesn't know it's coming and he's stood up. The guy's just an animal. He just gets up, keeps going after he gets hit."

Said Henry: "I just had to keep my head level, just help my offense. Do what I have to do, help us get a win and make plays."

Lost perhaps in all of Alabama's lofty statistics of the day was a 16-yard gain early in the fourth quarter. Facing a third-and-six at the Aggies' 24-yard line, Coker opted to keep the ball and run. After getting the first down he continued to run and instead of slipping safely out-of-bounds tucked his shoulder and delivered a blow to the Texas A&M cornerback, Nick Harvey. It was the latest show of toughness from Coker, who had already endeared himself to teammates and fans with similar runs.

A couple of days after the game, Coker disclosed some of the nicknames his teammates had given him for plays like this: Vanilla Vick and Cam Cracker. "It's getting a little out of hand," Coker said, smiling.

But there was no laughing about the task that remained for Alabama. "Everybody just realizes we have to win every game," Coker said. "Our backs are against the wall and you just have to perform out there. I don't think anybody looks at it as pressure. We just realize we can't relax."

Despite the dominating performance, there was plenty of room for improvement. Alabama gave up a 68-yard punt return for a touchdown in the second quarter, a 44-yard pass completion that set up another touchdown in the third quarter, and also suffered a blocked punt in the third quarter.

But, overall, it was a masterful defensive performance on the road. The Aggies only managed 32 yards rushing in the game, and Alabama's defensive front recorded six sacks.

"Everybody did their jobs," said Alabama linebacker Reggie Ragland.

For Nick Saban, the win was another obstacle overcome by a team that seemed to relish the challenge facing them.

"This was a great team win," Saban said. "We knew this was going to be a really tough game against a very good team, in a very difficult place to play. The players really responded well. We had a lot of guys play a lot of plays. It was hot. They got tired. They got their second wind. They kept competing and kept playing."

Offensively, the "plan coming in here was: we were going to try and run the ball. Keep the ball away from them as much as we could. Derrick Henry had a fabulous game. The offensive line did an outstanding job. On defense, we made some mistakes, gave up some plays, but I think the four interceptions were huge in the game. Three scores on defense is unprecedented, probably some kind of record."

Saban added: "You got to hand it to this team. You know this (Texas A&M) is the second team ranked in the top 10 that we beat on the road in some really tough places to play, so I think you've got to respect the competitive character of this team. My hat's off to them. They did a fantastic job today."

Like Georgia's Mark Richt before him, Texas A&M coach Kevlin Sumlin tried to make sense of a humiliating loss at home.

"When you play a quality football team like Alabama, your mistakes are amplified," Sumlin said. "Instead of balls just being on the ground, Alabama was returning them for touchdowns. You look at the game, that's 21 points right there. Alabama had a lot to do with the way we played. I thought the second half we had an opportunity there with the blocked punt. But they drove the ball, and then for whatever reason we could not get the ball in the end zone."

Next up for Alabama would be a home date with Tennessee. It would be Alabama's eighth consecutive game without an off week. The fatigue would be clearly evident when the Crimson Tide returned home to Bryant-Denny Stadium.

CHAPTER EIGHT
Fighting Through Fatigue

Alabama 19, Tennessee 14

October 24, 2015

Bryant-Denny Stadium/Tuscaloosa

WITH THE EXCEPTION OF AUBURN, there has traditionally been no more intense rivalry in Alabama football history than the one with the orange-clad team to the north, the Tennessee Volunteers. Yet, since Nick Saban's arrival in Tuscaloosa in 2007, it hadn't been much of a competitive rivalry. Alabama reeled off eight consecutive victories, all of them except one by double-digit margins, as Tennessee faded from SEC and national contention.

Alabama was favored to make it nine in a row, but this was clearly the best team Tennessee had fielded in recent years. The Volunteers, led by dual-threat quarterback Josh Dobbs, were coming to Tuscaloosa with a mediocre 3-3 record, but it was a deceiving one. Tennessee had lost those three games by a combined 12 points to Oklahoma, Florida, and Arkansas—and blown double-digit leads to each team in the process.

There was one other telling sign that foreshadowed a tougher-than-expected game: like Texas A&M on Alabama's schedule before them, Tennessee had a bye week before playing the Crimson Tide. That didn't seem to matter during Alabama's rout of the Aggies, but it would come into play this week. There would be no excuses, but clearly Alabama needed a break. It would finally get one in another week, but not before having to face a resurgent Tennessee team determined to make the rivalry relevant again.

"This is the best team they've had for a while," Saban pointed out five days before the game. He noted that Tennessee not only had a prolific offense, its defense was much stronger than in years past.

"They play hard. They're physical, and for the most part they've been hard to score on," Saban said.

Saturday's game would prove him right. This would be a struggle from start to finish, although it didn't exactly look that way early on. Alabama mounted a nine-play, 75-yard scoring drive capped by Derrick Henry's 20-yard, multiple tackle-breaking touchdown run through the heart of Tennessee's defense with 7:14 left in the first quarter. It was a dominant drive that left many of the 101,821 fans in the stadium with little doubt that this would be another Alabama rout over Tennessee.

But the Vols quickly answered with a ten-play, 75-yard drive of their own, aided by a pass interference penalty, and ending with an 11-yard pass from Dobbs to receiver Josh Smith in the corner of the end zone.

That would be all the scoring in a 7-7 first half, thanks to two stifling defenses that recorded three quarterback sacks each.

Alabama started the second half with a 12-play, 73-yard drive behind Henry's running and passes from Coker to Calvin Ridley, O.J. Howard, Richard Mullaney, and ArDarius Stewart. But the Tide stalled at Tennessee's 2-yard line, and settled for a 19-yard field goal from Adam Griffith. Griffith added a 28-yard field goal with 7:08 left in the fourth quarter, giving Alabama a 13-7 lead. While Griffith was on target with both field goals, Tennessee's Aaron Medley struggled, missing all three field goals he attempted.

For the moment, though, it didn't seem to matter, as Tennessee answered Alabama's field goal with a fast, four-play, 75-yard drive, including long pass completions of 27 yards to Josh Smith and 34 yards to Josh Malone. Running back Jalen Hurd took it the final 11 yards for a touchdown. An extra point gave Tennessee a 14-13 lead with 5:49 left in the game and a stadium full of nervous fans.

Alabama's season was on the line.

"How bad do you want to do something?" Saban had replied earlier in the week when asked what he had told his team when they had to overcome fatigue and adversity.

The coach, the players, and the fans were about to find out.

Down by one point with the clock running out, Alabama started its offensive possession on the Crimson Tide 29-yard line, 71 yards away from the Tennessee end zone. It didn't begin well. Jake Coker was forced out of the pocket and sacked for a two-yard loss. On the next play, however, Coker launched a 29-yard pass down the sideline to ArDarius Stewart, who made an acrobatic catch at the Vols' 44-yard line. (Stewart, having his best game as an Alabama player, would finish with six receptions for 114 yards.)

Following two short runs by Henry, Coker dropped back again and hit Calvin Ridley with a 15-yard pass, to the Vol 25.

The rest was up to Henry and his offensive line. Henry rushed for six yards, then five yards, and finally took off on a 14-yard touchdown run. Alabama took the lead at 19-14 with 2:24 left.

The Crimson Tide defense closed it out, shutting down Dobbs and the Tennessee offense, effectively ending the game when Alabama reserve linebacker Ryan Anderson stripped Dobbs of the ball. Big defensive tackle A'Shawn Robinson recovered it and took it back nine yards to the Tennessee 4.

Alabama had won its ninth consecutive game over the Vols, but this one had been anything but easy. Regardless, it was enough for Alabama players to light up cigars after the game—a tradition dating back to Paul "Bear" Bryant's era, when the legendary coach celebrated victories over Tennessee with cigars.

"Obviously that's a great win for our team," a relieved Saban said. "You know, we were tired out there today. Dead-legged, didn't look very quick. Didn't look very fast. Didn't have a lot of energy like we usually do. I think that's playing eight games in a row. But the best thing I can say is you've got to really respect guys . . . a team . . . that find a way to win. That makes plays when they have to make plays."

Alabama's Jake Coker, who was sacked six times but still managed to complete 21 of 27 passes for 247 yards, was joyous after what clearly was another game in which he continued to improve and evolve as a quarterback. His leadership during the final drive to complete a come-from-behind victory over arch-rival Tennessee would be something Alabama fans would be talking about for years to come.

"Every time I get to step out here is a dream come true, to be honest with you," Coker told *ESPN* immediately after the game. "But today is pretty special."

The mood was decidedly different in the Tennessee locker room.

"I thought our team showed some grit, some determination, some resiliency on the road against a very, very quality opponent, a top 10 opponent, in a hostile environment, and to drive the ball and put us in a position to win," Vol coach Butch Jones said. "But at the University of Tennessee there are no moral victories."

Ranked No. 8 and bound to move up, Alabama could now enjoy its first bye week of the season. Another classic matchup with LSU awaited in two weeks. The Tigers' much-heralded running back, Leonard Fournette, was the leading Heisman Trophy candidate, but Derrick Henry was beginning to draw widespread attention on his own. He had carried the ball 28 times for 143 yards and two touchdowns against Tennessee. And he would be asked to do even more against LSU.

For now, however, there was a victory to celebrate, and a moment, at least, to relax. The battle with LSU could wait.

"Obviously, this bye week is going to be very welcome to us in terms of getting some guys healed up and kind of getting rested up, so that we can maybe be at our best down the stretch," Saban said.

CHAPTER NINE
Running Away With It

Alabama 30, LSU 16

November 7, 2015

Bryant-Denny Stadium/Tuscaloosa

FOR MOST OF THE 2015 college football season, LSU running back Leonard Fournette was the runaway favorite to win the Heisman Trophy. At 6-foot-1, 230-pounds, Fournette not only had phenomenal agility and power, he was also one of the fastest players in college football.

The combination of speed and ability for such a large running back had made him one of the most highly recruited players in history in 2014, and Fournette had completely lived up to the hype.

Having rushed for more than 1,000 yards his freshman season, Fournette was now ripping through LSU's opponents as a sophomore. By the time he and his teammates arrived in Tuscaloosa for a showdown with Alabama on November 7, 2015, Fournette was on a record pace through seven games, with 1,352 rushing yards and an eye-opening 7.7-yards-per-carry average.

"Not only does he (Fournette) gain a record number of yards, he gains them with an almost cartoonish brutality," wrote Wright Thompson in an *ESPN: The Magazine* article a few days before the LSU-Alabama game. "He is becoming a football folk hero, like Bo or Herschel, Joe Namath, or LSU's only Heisman Trophy winner, Billy Cannon."

The problem for Fournette and LSU, however, was that their pro-style, running-downhill offense played right into Alabama's strengths. While the Crimson Tide had some well-known difficulty in the past adjusting defensively to spread, fast-paced offenses, they were entirely comfortable in slamming the door shut on more traditional attacks. LSU was coming to Tuscaloosa undefeated, at 7-0, but they were also about to face the best rushing defense in the nation.

And Alabama had its own big back with speed in Derrick Henry, who had just surpassed 1,000 yards rushing in eight games and was about to go on an unprecedented roll. It would begin with LSU, and by the time it was over it would be Henry, not Fournette, who was on a direct path to the Heisman Trophy.

The atmosphere at Bryant-Denny Stadium was reminiscent of what had been billed a "Game of the Century" back in 2011, when both teams had arrived unbeaten, ranked No. 1 and No. 2, and loaded with future NFL talent. That game became a titanic defensive struggle, won 9-6 in overtime by LSU.

This time the stakes were just as high, even if there was no "game of the century" hype. The first College Football Playoff rankings of the 2015 season had been released a few days earlier, with LSU at No. 2 and Alabama (7-1) at No. 4. The Crimson Tide had managed to overcome the Ole Miss loss and battle back to the forefront of college football. What's more, just before kick-off of Alabama-LSU, Ole Miss lost its second SEC game of the season when Arkansas, thanks to a bizarre and desperate lateral play, sent the game into overtime, then pulled out a 52-51 victory. The result meant that Alabama, not Ole Miss, now led the SEC West and controlled its own destiny.

But the Crimson Tide could not afford another loss if it was to repeat as SEC champions. LSU, having lost four consecutive games to Alabama, had its own challenge: the Tigers would have to find a way to get past their chief nemesis if they were to advance toward a championship.

For a quarter, at least, the game looked eerily similar to the 2011 contest, with neither team able to score. But there was one sign that the Crimson Tide was going to play this one to win, no matter the risk: On fourth-and-1 at the LSU 31-yard line, Alabama went for it instead of opting for what would have been a 48-yard field goal attempt. Jake Coker, however, was stopped on a quarterback draw, and LSU took over possession.

Early in the second quarter, Alabama took another chance, this time with Derrick Henry successfully converting a fourth-and-1 at LSU's 24-yard line. A few plays later, Alabama settled for a 22-yard Adam Griffith field goal and took a 3-0 lead.

All the while, Alabama's defense was swarming Fournette every time he touched the ball. By contrast, Henry was just getting revved up for the Tide. In the second quarter, he broke free on a 40-yard run, stiff-arming defenders as he went, and was finally stopped at LSU's 2-yard line. On the next play he scored, and Alabama took a 10-3 lead.

LSU came right back with a touchdown on its next possession, with a 40-yard pass from Brandon Harris to Travin Dural.

The score cut Alabama's lead to 10-7. The Tigers soon added a 39-yard field goal to tie the game at 10-10.

But Alabama was not done.

With only seconds left in the first half, the Tide lined up to punt on a fourth down from LSU's 37-yard line, but coach Nick Saban thought better of it, called a timeout, and called over his placekicker Adam Griffith.

"At first I didn't want to give them (LSU) the ball if we missed it there," Saban said later. "They complete one pass and then they've got a chance to kick a field goal. But I looked at Adam and I said, 'What do you think?' He said, 'I think I can hit it.' He got a little wind behind him, and he hit it good."

Said Griffith: "Good thing he trusts me. He asked me if I felt good about it. I was like, 'Yeah, sure.' He's like, 'OK, get out there.' And it was good."

Griffith's 55-yarder tied a record for the second longest field goal in Alabama's history, put the Tide up 13-10, and gave the team a lift going into halftime. More importantly, Alabama's defense had locked in on Leonard Fournette, holding him to just nine yards on nine carries, a shocking one-yard-per-carry average for a running back billed as the best in the nation.

Derrick Henry, by contrast, was having early success on LSU's defense, with 90 first-half yards and a touchdown on 15 carries. It would only get much better for Henry, and worse for LSU, in the second half.

Already buoyed by Griffith's long field goal to close the second quarter, Alabama's defense completely changed the game on the first play from scrimmage of the second half, when linebacker Dillon Lee intercepted LSU quarterback Brandon Harris's pass near the sideline, giving the Crimson Tide the ball at the Tigers' 28-yard line.

"It's something we needed right there coming out of the half, and re-establishing what we were trying to do," Lee said. "Everybody was really happy. I guess you could tell, everyone kept slapping me on my head."

Lee's coach, Saban, called it "maybe the turning point in the game."

Alabama quickly took advantage. A 25-yard Coker-to-Kenyan Drake pass gave the Crimson Tide a first down at the LSU 3. It took three consecutive runs by Henry, who finally took it into the end zone from a yard out. Alabama led 20-10 and was in control of the game.

Alabama would again turn to Henry, with key running plays from Drake, as well, to put LSU away. Henry's 7-yard touchdown run later in the third quarter gave the Tide a 27-10 cushion, and Griffith added another field goal, this one from 29 yards, to pad Alabama's lead to 30-10.

Henry would finish the most significant night in his Alabama career to that point with 210 yards and three touchdowns on 38 workhorse carries. His LSU counterpart, Fournette, was held to just 31 yards on 19 carries—a stunning turn of events that all but destroyed the LSU running back's Heisman chances and lifted Henry to frontrunner status.

"I'm not really worried about the Heisman," Henry said after the game, brushing off comparisons to Fournette. "We came out and played. We came out and competed. We beat a great team as a whole."

Henry made just one mistake during the game, a fumble early in the fourth quarter that gave LSU the ball at the Alabama 22. Moments later, Fournette got loose on his only significant run of the night, an 18-yarder, to move the ball down to the 4. He eventually took it in from the 1-yard line. Alabama blocked LSU's extra point attempt.

With a 30-16 lead and 9:18 left in the game, Alabama was forced to begin its next series from the Tide 4-yard line after an illegal block penalty on the kickoff return. It wouldn't matter. Coker and the offense again turned to Henry to drive the ball and run the clock. He and his teammates did just that, mounting a long, grinding drive that used up all of the time left and ended the game with the Tide at the LSU 16-yard line.

"I just wanted to finish the drive for us to secure the win," Henry said. "I wanted to keep the clock running, run physical, just so the time would run out for us to be able to get the win. LSU, every year they're a physical team. We knew it was going to be a physical game. A 15-round fight."

Alabama claimed its fifth consecutive victory over LSU, and Saban expressed pride in a team that was obviously earning his respect.

"I've always liked the grit of this team," Saban said. I've always liked the way this team competes. We haven't always executed right, and people can criticize the penalties and negative plays that we have sometimes, but the ability to overcome adversity has not been an issue with this group so far. Hopefully, we can continue to persevere."

Much of the talk after the game focused on Henry's success, and Fournette's struggles.

"Derrick, he did the same thing he's been doing," Jake Coker said. "For some reason he just doesn't get as much credit as the other guy (Fournette). The other guy's really good, too. I'm not going to take a shot at him at all. He's a great player. But so is that guy right there (Henry). He deserves every bit of credit that he's going to get."

Coker said he learned of Arkansas' victory over Ole Miss, which gave Alabama the lead in the SEC West, from his brother after the game.

"He said Arkansas pulled off some crazy game," Coker said. "I've just got to see it on TV."

But he was quick to add: "That's great news for us, but we've got Mississippi State next week."

For LSU, the night couldn't have gone worse. And the fallout seemed to linger. LSU would go on to lose its next two games, to Arkansas and Ole Miss. Fournette's Heisman campaign was not the only thing that had disappeared. LSU's season seemed to have disappeared with it. It didn't help LSU that *CBS*'s broadcast of the game drew the largest regular season television audience of the season up until that point.

The mood was somber when Tigers coach Les Miles met with reporters after the Alabama game.

"Congratulations to Alabama," he said. "I thought that they played very well, played pretty hard. We couldn't get on track offensively. . . . The offensive line faced a very talented, very capable defense line in Alabama. They were tested. Our runs weren't allowing us to get first downs."

Asked about Fournette, Miles said, "There's a lot of football left to play. It's not Leonard's fault. It's all of us."

CHAPTER TEN

Silencing the Cowbells

Alabama 31, Mississippi State 6

November 14, 2016

Davis Wade Stadium/Starkville

THE DECISIVE VICTORY OVER AN undefeated and second-ranked LSU team was a key turning point for Alabama, not only in practical terms—the Tide now stood atop the SEC West standings—but in public perception. The nation had seen a new superstar emerge in Derrick Henry and also watched as the odds-on-favorite to win the Heisman, Leonard Fournette, disappeared beneath a ferocious Alabama defense.

Such a difference one game had made.

Just a few days earlier, when the first CFB Playoff rankings of the season were released, there had been more than a few analysts claiming Alabama hadn't earned its place in the national championship discussion.

"Bama at 4 is definitely my biggest issue," *ESPN* analyst and former Florida State quarterback Danny Kanell said three days before the LSU game. "I think they are 100 percent graded on a different scale. They get more benefit of the doubt."

Kanell, viewed by many Tide fans as anti-Bama and anti-SEC, was not alone in his assessment. *USA Today*'s Dan Wolken, another frequent critic of the Crimson Tide, tweeted on November 3: "Seriously, it's the only program in the country that doesn't get penalized for losing a game. It's disgraceful."

Never mind that Alabama had fallen 10 spots, from No. 2 to No. 12 in the *Associated Press* and *USA Today*/Amway Coaches poll rankings after the Ole Miss loss. Perception, if not accuracy, was everything. What critics failed to notice, perhaps, was that the Tide had steadily earned its way back with difficult road trips, and dominant victories over Georgia in Athens and Texas A&M at College Station, while also taking care of Arkansas and Tennessee at home. That same Tennessee team had led highly regarded Oklahoma by 17-3 into the fourth quarter. The Vols were no pushover, as their record after the narrow Alabama loss would prove: Tennessee went undefeated the rest of the season and routed No. 12 Northwestern 45-6 in the Outback Bowl.

As for Alabama, the critics were simply disarmed after the LSU game. It was an undeniably impressive victory, had put Alabama back in the driver's seat in the SEC West, and was the kind of statement win no credible analyst could ignore.

Kanell, who had refused to put Alabama in his top 4 projections all season, finally ranked the Crimson Tide at No. 4. The only rankings that mattered, however, came from the College Football Playoff Selection Committee, which moved Alabama from No. 4 to No. 2, replacing LSU. Only Clemson, undefeated and scoring impressive victories in the Atlantic Coast Conference, was ranked higher.

Now it was on to Starkville, 80 miles up the road from Tuscaloosa, for a date with Mississippi State and a journey into the abyss of a stadium where the ear-shattering noise of clanging cowbells is not only allowed, but is as revered a tradition as there is in college football.

Against the Bulldogs, Alabama would be facing the SEC's best quarterback—three-year starter Dak Prescott, who had shattered the Mississippi State record book, accounting for more than 100 career touchdowns and running away with offensive records. A year earlier, in 2014, he had led his undefeated team into Tuscaloosa with the program's first-ever national No. 1 ranking, but a 25-20 loss ended that run. This time, the Bulldogs were 7-2 and ranked No. 17 but represented no less a threat, especially at home, to Alabama's bid to return to the college football playoffs.

Midway through the first quarter, it looked like Prescott might be on his way to avenging the crushing loss from 2014: he drove his team 50 yards, with a first-and-goal at the Alabama 3. But he couldn't complete the deal against the Crimson Tide's monstrous front seven, and the drive stalled with a turnover on downs at the Alabama 2-yard line.

The first quarter ended in a scoreless tie, with Jake Coker and his Alabama offense sputtering against Bulldog defenders, and the deafening roar of those infernal cowbells. But the game turned suddenly on a single play at the 10:44 mark in the second quarter, when the Crimson Tide's Cyrus Jones scored on a 69-yard punt return, bursting the dam open on what had been a stifling defensive game. Other big plays quickly followed, including a 60-yard Coker-to-Calvin Ridley touchdown throw, and a home-crowd-silencing, dramatic 74-yard touchdown run by Derrick Henry. Henry added an encore 65-yard touchdown run in the fourth quarter.

The Tide's 31-6 victory was yet another dominant road performance in the nation's best conference. The result was that Alabama remained on a direct path to the SEC title game and the national playoffs, but with plenty of obstacles still in the way.

For Henry, it was another 200-plus-yards rushing game (204 yards on 22 carries for a whopping 9.3-yards-per-carry average). The Heisman Trophy now seemed a very real possibility. Defensively, the Tide harassed Prescott the entire game, recording nine sacks—the most ever against the star quarterback—with Jonathan Allen, Ryan Anderson, A'Shawn Robinson, and Tim Williams each sharing the glory. And though they didn't record a sack, the Tide's Reuben Foster, with ten tackles, and Reggie Ragland, with eight, had impressive performances.

Even Nick Saban couldn't avoid his defensive unit's fury. During the game, Jonathan Allen, rushing from the sideline, ran into Saban, cutting and bruising the coach's left cheek.

"I was trying to run on the field, and coach Saban kind of got in the way, and we kind of collided," Allen said. "At the time I didn't notice it, but I saw a little gash on him, but he's a tough guy. He'll be all right. I just asked if he's OK, and he said, 'Good' and moved on. It's football."

Asked about it at his postgame news conference, Saban said, to laughter: "Well, I didn't play today. But those good pass rushers we always talk about . . . we knew that we were going to have to sub really, really fast. So when it was third down and we call 'dime rabbits,' those big guys come barreling off the sidelines. Well, Jonathan Allen barreled right into me one time. And the athlete that I am, I was able to keep my feet.

"The players were really concerned, but you know they don't make 'em like they used to," Saban added, slowly breaking into a smile.

As for his team's victory, Saban described it as "kind of a weird game, you know, where every touchdown was a big play."

The irony, and a little troubling, was that Mississippi State actually outgained Alabama with 393 total yards to 379. Despite spending much of the game on his back with those sacks, Prescott still managed to throw for 300 yards, but Bama's defense came through when it had to.

"Dak Prescott is a tough guy to defend," Saban said. "I know they gained a lot of yards today, but our defense did a really good job of not allowing a lot of points. Got them stopped inside the five, and a couple of times in the red zone, which I think is really, really important."

Despite the win, Alabama lost running back Kenyan Drake for the next couple of games with a fractured arm. Drake had missed most of the 2014 season after suffering a broken leg. And this was yet another setback. But given the advances in medical technology and his own determination, Drake would return from the injury in time to have a huge impact during Alabama's post-season run.

CHAPTER ELEVEN
A Tin Horn

Alabama 56, Charleston Southern 6

November 21, 2015

Bryant-Denny Stadium/Tuscaloosa

IT HAS BECOME AS PREDICTABLE as the freight trains that rumble daily over tracks just south of Alabama football's Thomas-Drew Practice Fields, snarling traffic, frustrating drivers, and ensuring that Tuscaloosa maintains vestiges of a small southern town atmosphere despite the skyrocketing recent growth of its state university.

We're talking, of course, about the lecture Nick Saban invariably unleashes when he thinks an opponent is being disrespected.

It was time.

Already, Saban had delivered a classic lecture back in September before the Middle Tennessee game. Yet, there was no way reporters were going to get through this week, with lower division Charleston Southern coming to town, without another Saban outburst.

Only this time Saban didn't need any particular reason to rev things up. At his mid-week news conference, he simply took a respectful question about Charleston Southern quarterback Austin Brown's past Division 1 experience (he had transferred from UAB) and rolled with it. What followed would be a tirade that not only revived an old 19th-century phrase—with profanity added—but pretty much broke the Internet in the process.

It played out like this: Saban—referring to the 9-1 Buccaneers, a good Football Championship Subdivision team—grasped the podium and slowly began to deliver his message, building up a sort of controlled indignation as he went: "These teams that are typically the best teams in their division are really good teams. You all may be taking the week off this week, but I'm not. And a lot of people take a lot of things for granted, and I get questions like, 'Well, how important is it for the young guys to get to play this week?' Well, how in the hell do you know they're going to get to play? What makes you think you can just assume that they're gonna get to play? Because you're assuming that the other team is not very good? They do have a Division 1 quarterback. He plays like a Division 1 quarterback and they're very, very productive on offense and they do a good job of executing what they do. And if we don't play good against them…"

Saban stopped momentarily in mid-sentence, shrugged, looked out over the group of reporters, and continued to let it fly, his voice spiraling: "Y'all don't remember the (2011) Georgia Southern game, do you? I don't think we had a guy on that field that didn't play in the NFL and about four or five of them were first-round draft picks. And I think that team won a national championship, but I'm not sure. And they (Georgia Southern) ran through our ass like shit through a tin horn, man, and we could not stop them. Could not stop 'em. Could not stop 'em!"

Immediately, the phrase "shit through a tin horn" was cascading through social media and sending the curious in search of the source of the phrase, which obviously referred to something that was so easily transported that it, as Saban repeatedly explained, couldn't be stopped.

There were a lot of explanations for the phrase, but the main ones centered on old adages like "mud through a tin horn" and "butter through a tin horn," originating in the 19th century and obviously finding their way into a lexicon used by the best college football coach in America.

Whatever the terminology, Saban's message was crystal clear: *If we overlook Charleston Southern, they might just do to us what Georgia Southern did back in 2011, run through us like shit through a tin horn.*

What Georgia Southern did not do in 2011, however, was defeat Alabama. The Tide won that game, 45-21, but Saban's point was made. The Golden Eagles had totaled 302 rushing yards and embarrassed a proud Alabama defense, the same defense that would later shut out LSU, 21-0, in the Bowl Championship Series national title game in New Orleans.

"I think we had given up like 300 yards rushing the whole season in ten games (leading up to Georgia Southern)," Saban said. "That's like 30 yards a game. And all anybody wanted to talk about was how dominant our front was, and nobody could run against us. They got 300 yards rushing in one game."

The news conference, as it turned out, was the gift that kept on giving. Georgia Southern's official Twitter football account posted this tweet the next day: "Thanks for the memories, Coach Saban." And T-shirts with Saban's quotes appeared immediately, doing brisk business on Georgia Southern's campus and elsewhere.

Almost lost in the tin horn talk was Saban's reference to marriage in the same news conference: "You know, everybody gets all excited about the beginning of the season. You get excited about getting married, all right. But after you're married for a while, you know, you've got to have a process to make it work. No matter what happens, we need to have a process to make it work in every game that we play. Every game that we play. You can't assume anything."

Alex Byington, a beat reporter for newspapers in Florence and Decatur, Alabama, tweeted: "The most underrated part of it all was his attempt at marriage advice."

Like most of Saban's lectures, this one seemed far more calculated than angry, and the point was made. There was a game to be played. Charleston Southern may be an FCS team, but they were a good one, and they stood in the way of preparations for the big Iron Bowl game that would follow in a week.

Alabama was a 38.5-point favorite over the Buccaneers, and even that, Charleston Southern coach Jamey Chadwell joked, might not be enough. On *The Paul Finebaum Show*, Chadwell said, "We can play our very best, Alabama could play their absolute worst, and it would probably still not be close."

Speaking of the betting line, Chadwell joked, "I'm surprised it's that low, to be honest with you. I might even take that bet."

As it turned out, he was right: a 50-point line would have been more accurate.

Alabama had little trouble with the Buccaneers, building a 49-0 halftime lead, emptying the bench, and winning the game, 56-6. While the game obviously would have little lasting historical significance, it was another victory in what was shaping up to be a magical season. A few records also fell in the process.

Cyrus Jones became the first Crimson Tide player ever to return two punts for touchdowns in a single game (scoring on runs of 43 and 72 yards), and Derrick Henry, with two scores, tied Trent Richardson's single-season school record of 21 touchdowns.

Henry sat out the entire second half, heading to the bench with just nine carries for 68 yards.

Ironically, Charleston Southern chose not to play its Division 1-experienced starting quarterback, Austin Brown, saving him for the FCS playoffs instead of subjecting him to a Bama defense that had sacked Mississippi State's Dak Prescott nine times a week earlier.

"The outcome was about what we expected," Chadwell said. "I was hoping we would put up a little more of a fight there in the first half. . . . Our main goal was to come in here and not get hurt, not get injured. I think we accomplished that. They're obviously a good team."

Saban, taking a far different tone with reporters after the game than he had earlier in the week, expressed satisfaction with his players' efforts.

"Sometimes we play a little lackluster in games like this, especially this time of year," he said. "I told them that if you're not inspired to play every play that you play, then you're kind of cheating yourself because it's about who you are, and how you compete. I certainly was pleased with the way we went out there and executed well."

Now it was on to Auburn, 160 miles to the southeast, and an Iron Bowl showdown in the same stadium where one of the most iconic plays in history, the "Kick-6," had blown the lid off the college football world and stunned a national television audience. The memory was still fresh.

CHAPTER TWELVE

Taking Care of Business—
The Iron Bowl/Alabama vs. Auburn

Alabama 29, Auburn 13

November 28, 2015

Jordan-Hare Stadium/Auburn

NICK SABAN'S EXTRAORDINARY SUCCESS IN nine seasons at Alabama had left more than a string of conference foes reeling from the onslaught. By late November 2015, the Crimson Tide owned nine-game winning streaks over Tennessee and Arkansas, eight consecutive victories over Mississippi State, five straight wins over LSU, and four over Florida, among others. Ole Miss had, indeed, won two consecutive games over Alabama, but Saban still held a 7-2 record against the Rebels since coming to Tuscaloosa.

Auburn, however, remained not only the Crimson Tide's chief rival, but also its chief nemesis—judging solely by the jaw-dropping nature of the Tide's last two losses to the Tigers. Saban's Bama teams still commanded a 5-3 record over Auburn. And several of those victories were blowouts. No matter, they tended to be overshadowed by the high-profile loses, including the 2010 Iron Bowl, when soon-to-be Heisman Trophy winner Cam Newton engineered a comeback from 24 points down to defeat Alabama in Bryant-Denny Stadium. It was a devastating loss.

And it wasn't the last.

In 2013, undefeated and top-ranked Alabama traveled to Auburn with a berth in the SEC Championship Game on the line. Alabama had won back-to-back national titles. So when the Tide lined up for a 57-yard field goal attempt to break a 28-28 tie with one second left in regulation, it seemed entirely possible that the team's magical run might, just might, include a walk-off long kick for victory on the road.

It did not, of course, turn out that way.

The kick, by Adam Griffith, fell short, was caught by Auburn running back Chris Davis in his own end zone, and returned 109 yards for a touchdown and a shocking 34-28 victory. The Kick Six, or the "Nightmare in Jordan-Hare" as Alabama's student newspaper, *The Crimson White*, headlined it, was instantly hailed as one of the greatest college football plays of all time.

Now, two years later, Alabama was returning to the scene of that crushing defeat. As if that weren't enough weight for Alabama players to bear in the days before the 2015 game, there was also the usual build-up to what is often considered the nation's most intense college football rivalry.

The Alabama-Auburn series isn't simply played out on the field. It is a 365-day-a-year topic of conversation, with an impact that reaches nearly every aspect of life within the state—and within families. Even the players are not immune to it.

"Sadly, my brother, he's an Auburn fan," Alabama senior inside linebacker Reggie Ragland said a few days before the Iron Bowl. "I don't talk to him during this week sometimes. I try to stay away from him. I know how he is. He loves to talk trash. Knowing him, he'll probably call me in the next couple of days, talking about Auburn, or something like that."

Ragland, from Madison, Alabama, grew up around the rivalry, but many others on the team were immersed in it only after they suited up for the Crimson Tide.

"People back home have the Ohio State-Michigan rivalry, which is a huge game in itself, but back in Ohio and Michigan you have NFL teams and pro sports," said senior center Ryan Kelly, from West Chester, Ohio. "Down here you don't have that, so this is all people have. It means a lot to a lot of people in the state. It's just a huge game for us. I know every person on this team knows the significance of this game."

Kelly, along with so many others on the Tide's roster, had been on the field that night two years earlier when Auburn's Jordan-Hare Stadium exploded in celebration, with students and fans rushing onto the field after Davis crossed the goal line with no time remaining.

"It was kind of a blur at the very end of it," Kelly said. "I just kind of walked off the field and that's all I want to talk about. It wasn't a great feeling, but a lot of guys were on this team then that were there, so you really don't forget something like that. It's not going to fuel how we play. We've got to go execute."

The memories were still vivid for players and fans, but part of Saban's "process" has been to replace emotion with intense preparation, focus, and determination. There would be no talk of revenge. And Bama had already settled the issue a year later, in 2014, when the Tide won a 55-44 shootout with Auburn in Bryant-Denny Stadium. That win sent Alabama to the SEC title game, where the Tide defeated Missouri and moved on to the college football playoff.

There was, however, the little matter of Auburn coach Gus Malzahn's 2015 preseason comments to *ESPN*, when he told the network, "We didn't score touchdowns in the red zone. We should have put 60 on them, and we didn't. . . . We let them off the hook, but we've got them at home this year."

Process or not, Alabama now had even more motivation, and more locker room material, courtesy of the jab from Auburn's head coach.

Now, two days after Thanksgiving, on a beautiful fall day, more than 87,000 people overflowed Jordan-Hare Stadium for the 80th renewal of a rivalry that began in 1893, but took a 41-year hiatus after 1907 when Alabama and Auburn bickered over offensive formations, travel expenses, the game's location, and other real or perceived grievances. Only when the State Legislature threatened to withhold funding from both schools did the series finally jump-start again in 1948.

The game now seemed to be entering a new phase of glory: four of the last six Iron Bowl winners had gone on to win the national championship, and five of the six winners had played in the title game.

This year, only Alabama, at 10-1 and ranked No. 2 in the nation, had the opportunity to play for a championship. Auburn, ranked No. 6 in the *AP* preseason poll and picked by many analysts to make the CFB playoffs, had suffered through a disappointing season, with five losses and very nearly a sixth before pulling out an overtime win over lower-division Jacksonville State.

But this was the Iron Bowl, and anything could happen, as 2013 had so emphatically proven. As if to underscore the point, Auburn jumped out to a 6-3 first-quarter lead in this 2015 version, and the offenses for both teams traded field goals in the second quarter until Alabama started slowly racking up yardage with Derrick Henry's running and Jake Coker's passing. Still, the Tide couldn't get into the end zone, taking a 12-6 lead on the strength of four Adam Griffith field goals, including a 50-yarder with 24 seconds left in the half. It had been Griffith, as a backup placekicker back in 2013, whose attempted field goal had led to that infamous Kick Six. Now, he was looking like the Iron Bowl's most valuable player. He would add a fifth field goal in the second half.

"I feel like everybody's talking about that too much—the Kick Six," Griffith told reporters after the game. "That's two years ago. It happened. No, I wasn't thinking about that at all. I'm just doing my job."

While Griffith was indeed doing his part, Henry was just getting started. He ended the first half with 102 yards on 16 carries. He would get a whopping 30 more touches in the second half, finishing with an Alabama record 46 carries for 271 yards and a touchdown in a 29-13 victory over a stubborn Auburn team. It was Henry's fourth 200-plus-yards game of the season and helped push him past the Alabama single-season rushing record, with 1,797 yards.

Henry's powerful, workhorse performance included 19 fourth-quarter carries, the last 14 of them amazingly on consecutive Crimson Tide plays from scrimmage. Henry's final carry was a 25-yard touchdown run with 26 seconds left in the game, giving him 17 consecutive games with a rushing touchdown, also an Alabama record.

"My hat's off to him as a competitor," Nick Saban said. "He really inspires everybody on our team, the way he competes and the way he plays. The toughness that he runs with, and spirit. What a spirit."

Saban, not known to throw around superlatives lightly, seemed genuinely impressed at this running back's durability and strength.

"You know, we really would like for somebody else to run the ball, but it got tough to take him out and he seems like he gets stronger as the game goes on," Saban said. "So, it's hard to take him out at the end. He's the go-to guy. He didn't want to come out. He wanted to go. He said he was good, and he certainly finished the game like we needed to."

Said Henry: "Like I've said, the ball isn't that heavy, so I was good and I'm just happy we got the win as a team."

Henry's performance moved him ever closer to a trip to New York and the Heisman Trophy ceremony, but first things first. The Auburn victory sealed the SEC West title for the Crimson Tide and cleared the way for a return trip to Atlanta to play Florida for the conference championship. Alabama, invoking the team's 24-hour rule, would have a day to celebrate the Iron Bowl win, and less than six days to get ready for the Gators.

It had been a full team effort to get to this point, winning ten consecutive games since the Ole Miss loss, including key SEC road-game victories.

"We had to stay locked in and stay focused," Henry said. "When we got that loss, we didn't want to lose any more, so we just kept working hard in practice and kept trying to get better week after week."

Henry had not been the only hero, of course, in the Tide's run-up to the SEC title game. Others, including Jake Coker and his receivers, along with the best rushing defense in the nation, had contributed. But for Coker, in particular, who had grown up in Mobile, Alabama, the Iron Bowl carried special significance. He had contributed mightily to the victory, including a sensational third-quarter play when he scrambled to escape two defenders and threw a 34-yard touchdown strike on the run to ArDarius Stewart in the end zone. It was one of only two Crimson Tide touchdowns on the day.

"I can't explain it," Coker said then, referring to the Auburn victory as "something I always looked forward to and dreamed of."

At his postgame news conference, Saban was asked to compare this victory with his last visit to Jordan-Hare, when the game had ended in disaster.

"I'm just happy for this team, and this day," he said. "That (2013) game will be something that I never ever forget, and that certainly wasn't Adam's fault. But he did a great job today, and I'm not just talking about making the field goals, but he was great on the kickoffs. He's really done a nice job of finishing the season for us. He certainly was as good as good as you could be today."

Others agreed, including Henry, who had made it a point to rush over and celebrate with Griffin after the 50-yard field goal at the end of the first half.

"Adam, he was clutch," Henry said. "Man, I'm just so happy for him. You know, Adam can make any type of kick because he does it in practice. He was very clutch. So exciting for him to have his kicks. We really needed them and he did a great job."

Now it was on to Atlanta.

"To win the (SEC) West is an accomplishment," Saban said. "To have the opportunity to play for the SEC championship against a very good Florida team is certainly an opportunity that this team deserves and has worked hard for. And it'll be a challenge for us, but I can't tell you how proud I am of our team and players and how they competed really all year long since the Ole Miss game. This was a tough one today, but they responded well in the things they needed to do to have success."

CHAPTER THIRTEEN
The SEC Championship

Alabama 29, Florida 15

December 5, 2015

The Georgia Dome/Atlanta

ATLANTA'S GEORGIA DOME, WITH ITS iconic towering cable-supported roof, sits 200 miles east of Tuscaloosa, but it had become as comfortable as a stroll down the block for Alabama's football program. Eight times since 2008 the Crimson Tide had played in the dome, and seven times they had won, all but once by double-digit margins. The only loss there in Nick Saban's tenure had been a 2008 SEC championship game setback to Florida, but the Tide had come back a year later and dominated Tim Tebow and the Gators, 32-13.

Three national championships and three SEC titles later, Bama was returning yet again, with an opportunity to make it back-to-back conference titles—the Tide had defeated Missouri, 42-13, to claim the 2014 trophy—and the even greater glory of a spot in the college football semifinals.

This year, it was No. 18 Florida making its own return to the game for the first time since 2009. The Gators had won the SEC East with a 7-1 conference record, 10-2 overall. But they were 18-point underdogs to Alabama just a week after suffering a 27-2 loss to archrival Florida State. That defeat had taken the Gators out of any playoff consideration and lowered the hype for this game. But the Gators still had one of the nation's top-ranked defenses, and, more important, stood in Alabama's way to the playoff semifinals.

There was also the added element of a sort of family battle between Saban and first-year Florida coach Jim McElwain, who had served with great success as Alabama's offensive coordinator from 2008–2011.

McElwain, a favorite with Alabama fans despite now leading the Gators, took it all with good humor, looking over Alabama's talent-loaded roster and proclaiming, "Not real excited about playing these creatures, but that's the way it goes."

Given Saban and Alabama's success, McElwain was asked at a news conference if he considered himself among SEC coaches who "have a Nick Saban problem." He quickly answered, "A Nick Saban problem? What's wrong with him?" The laughter set a light-hearted tone just a day before the big game, but everyone knew what was at stake.

For Derrick Henry, who had set a national high school career rushing record of 12,124 yards in Yulee, Florida, the game would be a homecoming of sorts on a neutral field. Henry had grown up a Gators fan but was now closing in on a Heisman Trophy as the featured running back for Alabama. He had repeatedly deflected questions about the award, but with Heisman ballots due two days after the game, his performance would either close the deal or open the door to other candidates, including Stanford all-purpose running back Christian McCaffrey and Clemson quarterback Deshaun Watson.

"Not worried about that," Henry said when asked yet again about the Heisman five days before the SEC title game. "Worried about Florida, who we're playing this week, and preparing for them so we can be ready for the SEC championship on Saturday."

The only real question was whether Henry's 46 carries in the game against Auburn had left him fatigued. One thing was for certain: Henry's final carry against Auburn had been a 25-yard touchdown run, and if there was any sign at all that he might be tired, he sure didn't show it.

Florida defenders expressed confidence they would be able to contain Henry by filling their gaps and hitting him hard early, not giving him space or momentum, and trying to stop him from getting stronger as the game went on.

"If we keep hitting him and doing our job throughout four quarters, I'm confident in my group," said Gators defensive end Jonathan Bullard, an early-round NFL draft prospect.

Alabama All-American linebacker Reggie Ragland, who routinely faced Henry in practice, gave the Gators a bit of advance warning about what they faced against the super-sized running back.

"Oh, it's a handful," Ragland said. "I'm used to it now, but for the most part any time Derrick runs the ball you've got to bring everything you've got, and you've got to hit him hard and gang tackle him. . . . 'Any' means I had to tackle the right way, wrap up on him, because if you don't wrap up, he'll break every tackle, and you can't arm tackle him. It's a very hard development level."

It was a development level, however, that Florida's defense seemed prepared to reach when the game started. As it had in several earlier games, Alabama's offense had trouble sustaining drives early. The Gators held the Tide to 38 total yards in the first quarter, and just three of those on the ground. Derrick Henry managed just 24 rushing yards in the quarter, with most of that negated by two big sacks to Jake Coker.

Alabama's special teams, however, rattled Florida with two first-quarter kick blocks, one on a punt, which led to a safety, and the other on a field-goal attempt. The 2-0 first quarter score looked more like something fans would have seen in Atlanta's Turner Field instead of the Georgia Dome. Early in the second quarter, the score changed quickly when the Gators' Antonio Callaway took a booming long punt from Bama's J.K. Scott and returned it 85 yards for the game's first touchdown.

"We knew it was going to be a dog fight," Alabama corner-back Cyrus Jones said later. "They weren't gonna come in here and lay down. It's just a typical SEC matchup. They always give us a great game."

Florida's lead, at 7-2, seemed to wake up Alabama's offense. The Tide drove 64 yards on the next possession, ending with a 28-yard field goal from Adam Griffith. A few minutes later, with the ball back again, Coker went deep on first down, throwing 55 yards to Calvin Ridley, who leaped for the ball between two Florida defenders and came down with the reception on the Gators' 3-yard line. One of those defenders was All-American Vernon Hargreaves, who figured to be an almost certain NFL first-round draft choice.

"I actually felt like I had him (Hargreaves) kind of beat, and the ball came a little short so I had to rebound," Ridley said. "I had to go up and get it."

Two plays later, Henry scored on a two-yard run, and Alabama took a 12-7 lead into the locker room at halftime. Florida's offense, meanwhile, had been completely unable to get anything going in the second quarter against a defense that harassed quarterback Treon Harris with three sacks totaling a loss of 28 yards.

The Gators overall managed just one yard of total offense in the second quarter.

Still, Florida had given Alabama all it could handle in the first half. But it would not last. It was clear from the Tide's opening drive of the third quarter that these two teams were far from evenly matched. Bama drove 65 yards in 12 plays to open the second half, using up nearly seven minutes in the process, capped by Coker's three-yard keeper for a touchdown. As for Derrick Henry, he was just getting started. By the time the game was over, he would deliver a Heisman-worthy performance, pounding the Gators' highly-rated defense for 189 rushing yards and a touchdown on 44 workhorse carries en route to Alabama's 29-15 victory. Along the way, he set a new SEC single-season rushing record, with 1,986 yards—shattering the mark set by Herschel Walker 34 years earlier.

Henry, a monstrously powerful running back on the field but entirely modest and sincere off of it, gave credit to his coaches and teammates for his history-making season.

"We're really like a family," he said. "The Ole Miss loss, when we lost, nobody really hung their head. Everybody came back and refocused, and wanted to get here, that's what we tried to do. I'm just proud of this team."

It was Alabama's second consecutive SEC title—and the program's 25th conference championship overall. More important in terms of the 2015 season, the Tide had punched its ticket to the second-ever College Football Playoffs. The only question was which team they would face in the semifinals, and whether the venue would be in Dallas or Miami. That would be answered the next morning.

While the attention largely focused on Henry's performance, other Crimson Tide players contributed to the title game victory. Coker's 204 yards passing not only included the 55-yard throw near the goal line to Ridley in the second quarter, but also two touchdown passes in the second half. On one of them, a 34-yard throw from Coker, ArDarius Stewart made a circus catch in the end zone over two Florida defensive backs, including the much-heralded Hargreaves.

"I had to jump. I had to get it," Stewart said in the locker room after the game. "I had to catch it at its highest point. That's what we're coached to do."

No matter that the Tide had won the SEC title in the Georgia Dome just a year earlier, there was nothing jaded about the Tide's celebration this time around. Bama players knew what they had accomplished, how far they had come, and what they had to do to continue this journey.

"It's historic. That's all I can say, it's historic," Stewart said. "It's gonna be around forever. Nothing they can take from us. I think you can tell from the Ole Miss game, to right after this game tonight, even though we came out a little rocky we picked up, trusted each other, and we made things happen."

Saban echoed his players' thoughts in putting the entire season in context.

"After the Ole Miss game, these players all said they wanted to be a different team. They wanted to do something special. And probably more than any team I've ever coached, I wanted to see those guys succeed today and win the second back-to-back SEC championship, and have an opportunity to get in the playoff."

And then, in an unusual bit of introspection for Saban, he went a step further, admitting that he, too, had his doubts after the early season loss.

"I don't think anybody (in the media) really thought after the Ole Miss game this team would wind up here," he said. "To be honest with you, I had some questions in my mind as to whether we'd wind up here."

There was, however, at least one bittersweet topic of conversation after the game for Crimson Tide players. Defensive coordinator Kirby Smart, who for years had helped Saban bring Alabama's program back to prominence, had accepted an offer to become head coach at his alma mater, Georgia, following the departure of Mark Richt. Smart had already informed the players, and the news had been reported in the media, though there had been no public announcement. Smart told the players he would stay with the Crimson Tide throughout the playoffs.

"It's any coach's job to be the head guy one day, and I'm just grateful for him that he gets to do it at his alma mater," Cyrus Jones said. "He graduated from there, and I just wish the best for him."

Smart's defense had played a huge role in getting to Tide back to Atlanta. Against Florida, they gave up just 15 yards rushing, and 180 yards total offense. Alabama, by comparison, totaled 437 yards on offense. But it had not been easy, especially in the first half.

"It's the best defense that we faced," Henry said. "They're very physical, very disruptive, very fast on the defensive line. Athletic linebackers who are very physical and try to knock you out, and a good secondary."

But not good enough to stop Henry. Exactly one week later he would be in New York City, sitting in the front row at the Heisman Memorial Trophy ceremony, awaiting an announcement that would etch his name in college football history.

CHAPTER FOURTEEN

The Road to New York:
Derrick Henry Wins the Heisman

It was that moment in a blowout football game when the clock isn't running fast enough to catch up with fans walking toward the exits. When boredom has replaced drama. When the last hot dogs have been sold, and families lucky enough to get seats together are talking more about traffic leaving the stadium than about any action inside it.

On the field, however, the coaches, players, and officials are not done. Even if they would like to be. Not on this night.

It was October 19, 2013, and this was a yawner of a football game as the clock fell below two minutes at Alabama's Bryant-Denny Stadium. The Crimson Tide led Arkansas, 45-0, and there was little left to do but run the ball and watch the seconds disappear. Already, Nick Saban and his assistant coaches had emptied the bench, playing everyone with a helmet and shoulder pads.

One of the backups, Derrick Henry, the big, fast freshman running back who had been a national high school sensation, had received fewer than a handful of carries as the game wound down. Four other Alabama backs—T.J. Yeldon, Kenyan Drake, Jalston Fowler, and Dee Hart—had entered the game before Henry.

Now, in mop-up duty, Henry took a handoff from backup quarterback Blake Sims on first down and rushed five yards into the pile of bodies in front of him, stretching the ball to the Crimson Tide's 20-yard line. The clock continued to run. No one, least of all Arkansas, which wanted no more of this torture, had any notion of stopping the clock.

So Bama lined up again on second down, and everyone in the stadium knew it would be another handoff. Saban would never allow the Tide to throw a pass with this kind of lead so late in the game. Critics have said a lot of not-so-nice things about him, but running up the score is not one of them. Saban always respected the opponent, and the Tide was probably one more play away from taking a knee, then heading for the locker room.

Only, it didn't turn out that way.

Henry took the second-down handoff with 1:15 left in the game, cut back toward the left corner, and raced down the sideline, with Arkansas defenders helplessly in pursuit behind him.

"Two hundred thirty-eight pounds and 80 yards. Touchdown! Whoa!" *ESPN* play-by-play announcer Brad Nessler told his audience, adding moments later, "Holy smokes. A two-play drive, 80 of which is the freshman from Yulee, Florida, and he looked like he was heading to Florida down the sideline. Man, oh man."

It was the first touchdown of Henry's career at Alabama, and it was a spectacular one, ending the scoring (with an extra point added) at 52-0. "It shouldn't be possible for someone that large to fun that fast," said Marc Torrence, who was standing on the sideline as a sportswriter for *The Crimson White*, the student newspaper, when Henry swept by on his way to the end zone.

There would be many more jaw-dropping runs to follow for the 6-foot-3, 238-pound running back. Before he was done at Alabama, Henry would shatter many of the school's rushing and scoring records, and break a few SEC records along the way, including the conference's single-season rushing record held by the legendary Herschel Walker.

But on the night of the Arkansas game in 2013, no one could be sure just how far he would go. Henry had gained widespread attention as a high school recruit, setting a national high school rushing record of 12,124 yards at Yulee High School, where he was also a sprinter on the track team. His combination of speed, size, and power was rare.

He graduated early, enrolled at the University of Alabama in January 2013, and was doing well in spring practice before fracturing his fibula in a scrimmage, an injury that sidelined him through the summer, but clearly was in the rear-view mirror by the time Henry lined up against Arkansas later that season. His bigger problem, perhaps, was simply the talented roster of running backs at Alabama, where an apprentice sort of platoon system had been used since Saban's arrival, to great success.

One of the backs ahead of Henry on the depth chart was Kenyan Drake, who didn't let what became a defining moment in Henry's early Alabama career—the touchdown against Arkansas—pass without notice.

"I'm one of Derrick's biggest fans," Drake said after the game. "That's his favorite thing, to hit the outside corner. I always tell him, 'When you do it, I know you're going to show your speed, so just don't let anyone catch you from behind.' He sure didn't do that."

Nor did he do it any other day. No one was going to catch Henry once he got behind the defense. Long, breakaway runs would become a signature of his Alabama career. The only thing that could stop him, it seemed, was not being on the field. Henry had just 36 carries his freshman season. Two years later there would be *single games* when he had more carries than that. No matter, that first year he made the most of those carries, gaining 382 yards for an impressive 10.6 yards-per-carry average.

Still, for a five-star recruit who had been named *Parade Magazine's* Player of the Year and Florida's Mr. Football his senior year in high school, Henry's first season at Alabama had been long and frustrating. *ESPN* reported that Henry had even quietly contemplated transferring from Alabama but was urged by family and former high school coaches to stick it out, and at least talk to Alabama coaches about it. Whatever the outcome of those conversations in mid-December 2013, it was obvious that things turned around quickly for Henry when Alabama took the field against Oklahoma on January 2, 2014. Henry was given the No. 2 running back position, and he made the most of it, with 161 all-purpose yards and two touchdowns. Those included a 43-yard scoring run in the third quarter and a 61-yard TD in the fourth, when he took a short pass from AJ McCarron, cut through the Sooner defense, and then outran them to the end zone. Alabama lost the game, but Henry had made his mark.

"We decided that he was our second best back going into the this game, and we were going to give him an opportunity based on his performance in practice and what he had done, the confidence that he had gained throughout the course of the season in terms of knowing what to do and playing fast," Saban said after the game. "He certainly had an outstanding game tonight, and did a really good job for us, and I think he has a bright future."

As the 2014 season began, Henry, in his sophomore year, was still the No. 2 running back to Yeldon, but by the end of the year it was Henry who led all Crimson Tide rushers with 990 yards and 11 touchdowns, although Yeldon was right behind with 979 yards and an equal 11 TDs. If anything, sharing carries with such a talented running back as Yeldon had helped Henry, not only in his running technique and blocking ability, but also in keeping him fresh for what would be a phenomenal junior season.

Yet, the 2014 season had ended just as 2013, with another crushing loss in the Sugar Bowl. This time it was to Ohio State in the first-ever College Football playoff. Henry, however, had done his part, with 95 yards on 13 carries, a touchdown, and another 54 yards receiving. But Ohio State's running back Ezekiel Elliott had a far bigger game, with 230 yards on 20 carries, and two touchdowns, and his team won the game, 42-35.

Ohio State would go on to win the national championship in a blowout over Oregon and would be an overwhelming favorite to repeat in 2015. But as college football prognostications often go, the one regarding the Buckeyes' invincibility wouldn't pan out. Ohio State entered the 2015 season as a unanimous No. 1 choice in preseason polls. But Alabama, not the Buckeyes, would be there in the playoffs again in the postseason.

First, however, there was a lot of football to be played, and for the Crimson Tide Derrick Henry would be at the center of it.

Now, as the featured back with Yeldon off to the NFL, Henry went to work, beginning with 147 yards on just 13 carries and three touchdowns in the Crimson Tide's season opener against Wisconsin. Kenyan Drake, now Henry's backup, had suffered a broken leg early in the 2014 season, and there were lingering questions about how durable he would be in 2015. He answered those doubts with 77 yards rushing, a touchdown, and 48 yards receiving against the Badgers.

Together Henry and Drake would be a challenging tandem for defenses. But as the season progressed, Henry's workload increased. He was simply running over, around, and through SEC defenses. When he rushed for 210 yards and three touchdowns against LSU on November 7—and the Crimson Tide's defense held the Tigers' Leonard Fournette to just 39 yards on 19 carries—the Heisman Trophy race flipped on its end. Fournette had been a runaway favorite to win the trophy. Now Henry was the favorite, and Fournette's opportunity was done. At least for 2015.

"I'm not really worried about the Heisman," Henry said immediately after the LSU game. "I'm saying that we came out and played. We came out and competed and we beat a great team."

Henry had carried the ball 38 times against LSU. A week later, when Kenyan Drake suffered another injury, this time a broken arm against Mississippi State, Alabama's offense depended more than ever on Henry. He seemed more than up to the challenge. Obsessed with preparation in workouts and practice, Henry only got stronger down the stretch.

He gained 204 yards with two touchdowns against Mississippi State, played sparingly in the next game against Charleston Southern, carried the ball an eye-opening 46 times for 271 yards and a touchdown against Auburn, then added 189 yards and a touchdown on 44 carries against Florida in the SEC title game.

"I can't tell you how proud I am of this guy," Saban said, sitting next to Henry at a news conference after the Florida game. "He's had a phenomenal season, and he deserves every accolade that anyone could ever throw his way."

But was it enough as Heisman voters cast their ballots? Henry broke Herschel Walker's SEC single-season rushing record during the SEC championship game, with 1,986 yards. (Walker rushed for 1,891 yards in 1981.) And Henry's yards had come against eight of the top 50 rushing defenses in the nation. In fact, he had performed his best work against the best—rushing for an average 180 yards per game against the seven ranked opponents Alabama had faced so far. There were other superlatives, as well, including 23 touchdowns, tying the SEC single-season record, and a nation-leading 18 consecutive games with a rushing touchdown.

Late in the day on Monday, December 7, two days after the Florida game, it was announced that Henry, Stanford's all-purpose running back Christian McCaffrey, and Clemson quarterback

Deshaun Watson would be heading to New York as Heisman finalists.

Both Henry and Watson would also be heading to the college football playoffs. Clemson, at No. 1, would face No. 4 Oklahoma. And Alabama, ranked second, would face No. 3 Michigan State.

Finally, Henry could take a break from practice and preparation and enjoy the moment.

Winning the Heisman had "always been a dream of mine, so to just be in the conversation with this award is a blessing," Henry told reporters after the announcement. "It's a blessing to have this opportunity to play for this great university, for my teammates and coaches, and to just go out there and play on Saturdays."

The first stop for all three Heisman finalists would be at the College Football Hall of Fame in Atlanta, site of the 25th annual Home Depot College Football Awards on Thursday, December 10.

It was Derrick Henry's night.

He picked up all three awards for which he was a finalist, including the Maxwell Award as college football's player of the year, the Walter Camp Player of the Year Award, and the Doak Walker Award as the nation's best running back. Watson won the Davey O'Brien Award as the nation's top quarterback.

It was on to New York, and for Saturday evening, December 12.

Born to teenage parents, Henry had been raised in Yulee, Florida, by his grandmother, Gladys Henry, who had nicknamed him "Shocka" at his birth. After all, Derrick's parents were just 15 and 16 when he was born, and Shocka seemed to be appropriate. It was a nickname that would stick with Derrick Henry throughout his childhood.

Now 81, Gladys Henry was confined to a hospital bed in Jacksonville, Florida, and couldn't make the trip with Henry to New York. But she and a host of family members were watching *ESPN*'s live broadcast of the ceremony, and the room erupted with cheers when Henry was named the 81st winner of the Heisman Trophy.

In attendance at the ceremony were Henry's parents, Stacy Veal and Derrick Henry Sr., Alabama head coach Nick Saban, and running backs coach Burton Burns, among others. Derrick Henry, dapper for this primetime moment in a smart blue suit and crimson-striped tie, gave them all a hug before making his way to the podium for an emotional acceptance speech.

"Mom and Dad, man, my mom, my best friend who brought me into this world, I just want to thank you so much for always being there for me," Henry said, peering past the microphone at his mother, Stacy Veal. "Through my struggles you always heard me. Anytime I was struggling, you were always there for me. I'd call you late at night, you'd be asleep. I know you'd have to be up at 3 o'clock in the morning, but you would answer for me, just to hear what I had to say, and help me get through whatever I would need to get through. To my dad, my No. 1 fan, man, always kept me in sports. Always there for me, day after day, being young and being so supportive, keeping me in sports, I just want to thank you so much, man. Even in the games, every game I played, you was always loud."

Then he turned his thoughts to Gladys Henry, in that hospital bed in Jacksonville, surrounded by family.

"My grandmother, the woman who made me what I am today, I want to thank you so much," Henry said. "Even though you can't be here today, I feel you in spirit, and I love you so much. You made me who I am today. Hard work, dedication, and just doing what I wanted to do. You always told me, 'Always keep God first, pray,' and that I'd always make it far. I just want you to know much I love you and I'm praying for you."

Next, he addressed the people with whom he had spent the better part of three years at the University of Alabama.

"To my teammates, my brothers, my family, and the boys I love the most, you know coming into Alabama from Florida, they all accepted me, they all loved me and all supported me," he said. "And this season, man, they've seen me as a leader, taken me as a leader. My offensive line, if I could have had them here, I would have brought them all. They work so hard for me, they take pride in controlling the line of scrimmage, making sure I have success, and through this year, looking at these guys, the courage they had in me, the faith they had in me, I knew I couldn't let them down."

Henry went on to thank all of his coaches, both at Alabama and back in Yulee. His words to Saban underscored why so many talented recruits continued to line up to play for the man considered the best coach in America.

"You're a loyal coach," Henry said. "You always challenge us. I just love you coach, man. Without you, I wouldn't be here today."

Henry would go on to play two more games at Alabama before he opted to enter the NFL draft early as a junior. He would leave with a national championship, two SEC titles, and his name all over the Alabama record books.

Henry's performances against Michigan State and Clemson expanded his SEC single-season rushing record to 2,219 yards and 28 touchdowns. His 3,591 total career yards would also eclipse a school record, along with the 20 consecutive games in which he scored at least one touchdown.

Shortly before the Cotton Bowl battle with Michigan State, Alabama offense coordinator Lane Kiffin was asked why Henry was having such a record-breaking year.

"None of us thought this was going to happen," Kiffin said. "It's two things. The first thing is Derrick. He's unique. They just don't make guys that big, that fast, that tough. They just don't. That's genetics and work ethic. The second thing was injuries to Kenyan Drake. And so, I don't think the numbers would be where they were had Kenyan not been injured. They'd still be up there, but I think there would be some balance in there."

As for all those carries for Henry, Kiffin said, "I was always a 20-25 carry (coach). You worry about ball security because that's

where the fumbles increase. And so it just blows me away sometimes. I ask them upstairs on the headset, where he's (Henry) at.
He's at 30, he's at 36, at 38 carries, but it doesn't seem like it. It
doesn't even seem like you're giving him the ball that much. It
doesn't seem like he's wearing down. You're down there to see the
body language and to see where he is. We both (Saban and Kiffin)
talk all the time about taking him out, but no reason to."

Indeed. As Henry had said after carrying the ball 46 times for
271 yards in Alabama's 29-13 victory over Auburn: "The ball isn't
that heavy, so I was good."

CHAPTER FIFTEEN
Back to Work

Goodyear Cotton Bowl Classic

College Football Playoff Semifinal

Alabama 38, Michigan State 0

December 31, 2015

AT&T Stadium/Arlington, Texas

IT HAD BEEN A WHIRLWIND awards week, capped by the trip to New York City, with its accompanying national media blitz and the never-ending interviews and photo ops that go with winning a Heisman Trophy. Derrick Henry had handled it well, with genuine humility and a quiet dignity that he seemed to carry as easily as a football.

Nevertheless, by the time he and his teammates returned to practice in Tuscaloosa on December 16, Henry was ready to move on. Michigan State and a playoff semifinal awaited. When a reporter asked him after practice if the New York trip had been fun, Henry's frustration was evident.

"It was fun. I really don't want to talk about the Heisman stuff, " he said. "I want to focus on what we need to do to get ready for Michigan State. So if y'all can talk about that, I'd be happy. What happened is over with. I'm just trying to get back to what we need to do."

Usually affable and patient during interviews, Henry's mood didn't get any better when he was asked if it was difficult to focus with the holidays coming up.

"No, it's not difficult," he said with a quizzical look. "Why would it be difficult? We want to win a championship, so it's not difficult."

He lightened up immediately when the subject changed to his upfront blockers, who earlier that day won college football's inaugural Joe Moore Award as the nation's best offensive line. Already, Ryan Kelly had been awarded the Rimington Trophy as the nation's best center.

"They worked hard all year, competed every day, and did a great job for me," Henry said. "I credit all my success to them, man. I love those guys. I was just happy to see them get that award because they deserved it."

Later that evening, Henry took the entire offensive line out to dinner to thank them for their role in his record-breaking season, and the team's success.

At 12-1 and ranked No. 2, the SEC champions would face No. 3 Michigan State in the Cotton Bowl on New Year's Eve at AT&T Stadium in Arlington, Texas, home of the Dallas Cowboys. The winner would advance to the national championship game

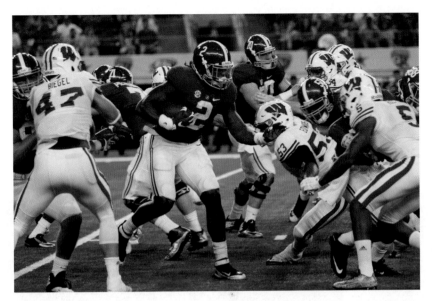

Derrick Henry in heavy traffic against Wisconsin in the season opener at AT&T Stadium in Arlington, Texas on September 5, 2015. Alabama defeated the Badgers 35–17.

Big Al waves the University of Alabama's script "A" flag after a Crimson Tide touchdown against Middle Tennessee State at Bryant-Denny Stadium on September 12, 2015.

Kenyan Drake tries to get past two Middle Tennessee State defenders after catching a short pass from Jake Coker in the first quarter.

Ole Miss receiver Quincy Adeboyejo races 66 yards to the end zone after catching a deflected pass in the third quarter against Alabama. The fluke play added to the Crimson Tide's misery on a night the team and its fans would like to forget.

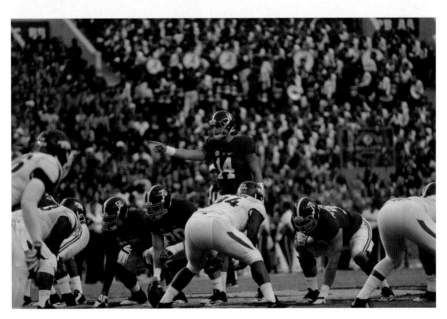

Jake Coker calls a play during Alabama's homecoming game against Arkansas on October 10, 2015.

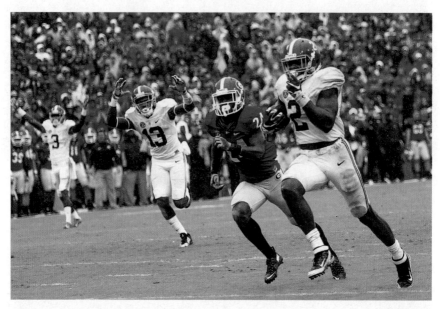

ArDarius Stewart (13) and Calvin Ridley (3) raise their arms in touchdown signals as Derrick Henry runs past Georgia defenders in the rain for a 30-yard score in the second quarter. Alabama defeated the Bulldogs 38–10 in Athens in a game that set the tone for the remainder of the season.

Freshman Mason Johnston marches with his trombone during the 2015 Homecoming pre-game performance.

Derrick Henry in the end zone after a 20-yard run for a touchdown in the first quarter against Tennessee.

Nick Saban confers with his coaches during the Tennessee game in Bryant–Denny Stadium. Alabama had to come from behind with a late fourth-quarter drive to defeat the Vols 19–14.

Tight end O.J. Howard is out of bounds at the Tennessee 1-yard line after a 7-yard reception in the third quarter.

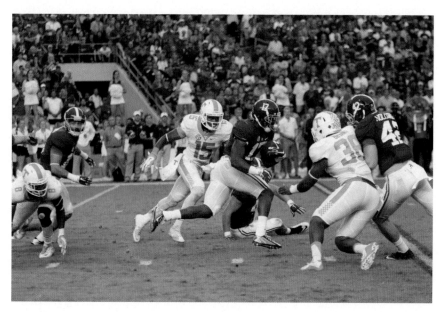

Kenyan Drake cuts through Tennessee defenders on a 29-yard kickoff return in the fourth quarter.

Derrick Henry rushes into the heart of Tennessee's defense during a bruising battle with the Vols on October 24, 2015.

Students celebrate a victory over Tennessee with an Alabama tradition—smoking cigars after a win over the Vols.

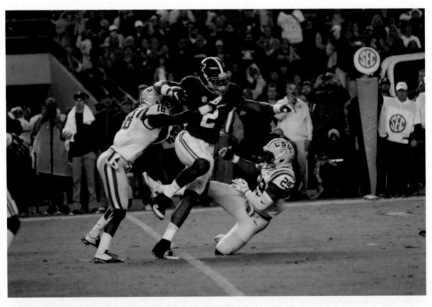

Derrick Henry strikes the Heisman pose during a run against LSU on November 7, 2015. Henry gained 210 yards on 38 carries in a game that flipped the Heisman Trophy race in his favor, and all but closed the door on LSU running back Leonard Fournette's chances for the trophy in 2015.

Cyrus Jones stretches before the game against Mississippi State.

Cyrus Jones takes a punt back 69 yards for a touchdown in the second quarter against Mississippi State in Starkville on November 14, 2015.

Derrick Henry celebrates with teammate Ross Pierschbacher after running a touchdown in the first quarter against Charleston Southern.

Cyrus Jones celebrates after a 72-yard punt return for a touchdown against Charleston Southern.

Jake Coker goes to the air against Auburn after a play-action fake to Derrick Henry. Alabama won the Iron Bowl 29-13.

Coach Nick Saban, Derrick Henry and the Crimson Tide celebrate their back-to-back SEC Championship victory on December 5, 2015. With the 29-15 win over Florida at the Georgia Dome in Atlanta, Alabama punched its ticket to the national playoff semifinal in the Cotton Bowl against Michigan State.

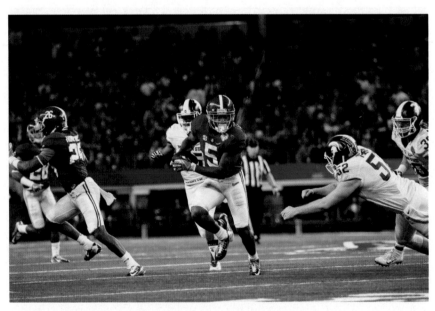

Cyrus Jones scores a touchdown on a 57-yard punt return in the third quarter of the Cotton Bowl playoff semifinal game against Michigan State.

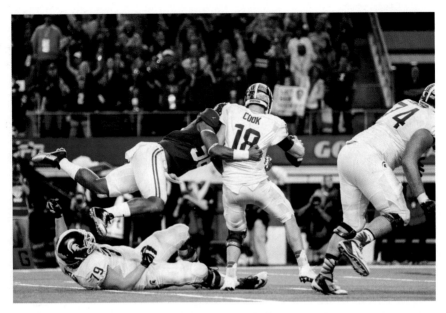

Alabama's Tim Williams flies into Connor Cook, sacking the Michigan State quarterback for a 10-yard loss in the Cotton Bowl.

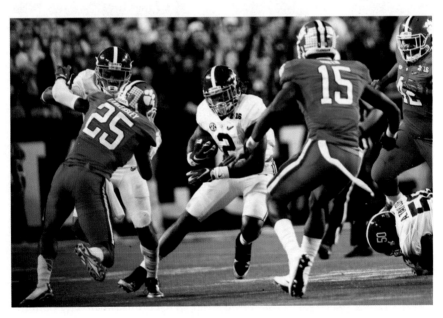

Derrick Henry runs the ball against Clemson in the first quarter of the College Football Playoff National Championship Game in Glendale, Arizona.

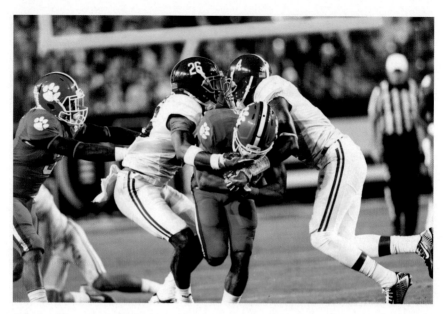

Marlon Humphrey (26) and Eddie Jackson (4) bring down Clemson's Zac Brooks after a gain of 22 yards.

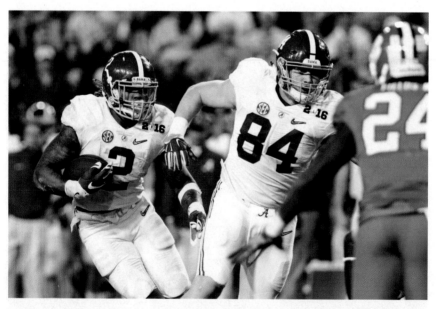

Derrick Henry and tight end Hale Hentges face off against Clemson's defense late in the fourth quarter of the national title game.

Marlon Humphrey celebrates with teammates after recovering a crucial onside kick in the fourth quarter of the CFP National Championship Game.

Nick Saban and the Crimson Tide with the CFP National Championship trophy after Alabama's thrilling 45–40 victory over Clemson.

in Glendale, Arizona, 11 days later to face the winner of No. 1 Clemson versus No. 4 Oklahoma in the Orange Bowl.

Nearly 800 miles north of Tuscaloosa, Michigan State, 12-1 on the season and Big 10 champion, was just beginning its own preparations in East Lansing. Much of that work, it seemed, focused on stopping Derrick Henry.

Spartan linebackers Riley Bullough and Jon Reschke had both addressed tweets to Henry just after the Heisman ceremony: "Congrats, @KingHenry_21! Excited to play against a heisman winner! Hopefully you don't think me and @J_Reschke33 are that weird but oh well," Bullough tweeted. And Reschke used even fewer characters, but his meaning was clear: "can't wait Derrick!"

The tweets were good-natured but also clearly underscored Michigan State's confidence that they could match up with Alabama. After all, the Spartans had held Ohio State to just 132 total yards in its own stadium in defeating the Buckeyes, 17-14. Ohio State's Ezekiel Elliott, one of the nation's best running backs, had gotten just 33 yards, though he would later complain that he should have touched the ball more than the 12 carries he had.

Reschke, for his part, had won the Walter Camp National Defensive Player of the Week for his efforts against Ohio State— and it was obvious that he, Bullough, and the other Michigan State defenders were determined to have a similar performance against Alabama and Henry.

The Spartans made no secret about their defensive game plan.

"Well, Coker, he's a game manager. He does a great job," Bullough said during a news conference after both teams arrived in Dallas for final preparations. "Talking defensively, what we want to do is stop the run. That's kind of what we want to do each and every week, especially this week going against Derrick Henry and that Alabama offensive line. So we feel like if we can take away the run as best we can, and put the game in Coker's hand to throw it, you know, that's what we really want to do."

There it was: "… put the game in Coker's hand to throw it…"

Although some analysts would later insinuate that Bullough's comments showed a lack of respect to Coker, it was more like the Michigan State linebacker was simply being honest. If the Spartans couldn't stop Henry, they had no chance against Alabama. Stopping him, and making Coker throw downfield, was their only hope. As it turned out, they had no chance anyway.

Once the game started, the Spartans, with one of the nation's top 10 rushing defenses, did what they had said they would do against Henry. They brought their linebackers up to fill the gaps, loaded the box, and held the Heisman Trophy winner to 75 yards on 20 carries. In short, they did, indeed, put the game in Coker's hands. The problem for Michigan State is that Coker was more than ready for the challenge. He shredded the Spartans, completing 25 of 30 passes for 286 yards and two touchdowns, with big plays all over the field. Alabama's defense did the rest, sacking MSU's talented quarterback, Connor Cook, four times and forcing him out of the pocket so relentlessly that he could be seen on the stadium's huge video screen in the third quarter clearly saying, "They're f..king everywhere."

And they were.

The Crimson Tide routed Michigan State, 38-0, handing the Spartans their first shutout in 15 years and earning a spot in the national championship final opposite No. 1 Clemson, which a few hours earlier used an explosive offense, and its own tenacious defense, to wallop No. 4 Oklahoma, 37-17, in the Orange Bowl.

That set up be an intriguing match between Saban and Clemson head coach Dabo Swinney, a former Alabama player and assistant coach who remained a favorite among many Crimson Tide fans. For now, however, there were victories for both Saban and Sweeney to celebrate with their teams as the year 2015 ended with confetti flying in Dallas and Miami.

Saban sidestepped questions about whether he thought his quarterback had been underestimated but noted he certainly wasn't surprised by Coker's performance.

'He's pretty much done a good job all year long in terms of what we've asked him to do," Saban said. "He's not a selfish guy at all. . . . Tonight he had to make the plays because they were there, and he certainly made them. But I think in each game that we've asked him to do that, he's come through nicely for us."

Coker, of course, didn't do it alone. Although it wasn't Henry's biggest night of the season, he still scored two touchdowns—including a jaw dropping 11-yarder in which his stiff-arm flipped the Spartans' All-Big 10 defensive end Shilique Calhoun to the ground—and helped open up Alabama's passing game by forcing Michigan State into single coverage.

Calhoun, who otherwise played well for MSU, gave credit where credit was due after the game.

"I think they have a versatile offense where they're not only able to score with their back, but they do a great job of getting their receivers out and putting them in situations where they can make plays," he said. "No, I wouldn't have guessed the game to be in this situation where they win by what they did with his (Henry's) yardage. But at the same time . . . credit the Alabama football team. They did a great job of finding weak spots and capitalizing on those moments."

Overall, Alabama's offense, aided by those timely big plays, managed 440 total yards to just 239 for the Spartans (and just 29 of that rushing). It was Michigan State's worst offensive performance of the season.

For a while, though, it looked like it might not be much better for Alabama. The first quarter had ended in a tie. But that changed in seconds with just over six minutes left in the second quarter, when Coker launched a perfect deep strike for 50 yards to Calvin Ridley at the MSU 1-yard line. Henry scored two plays later, and

Alabama had a lead that would be all it would need, given the shutout in the making. But the Crimson Tide was far from done. Ridley, a freshman who by now was looking like the Tide's next Amari Cooper, would finish the game with eight receptions for 138 yards and two third-quarter touchdowns. These included a sensational six-yard catch near the out-of-bounds line in the end zone with a defender in his face, and another 50-yard strike from Coker, this one perfectly leading Ridley into the end zone.

The game also marked a return, of sorts, for Alabama's big, speedy tight end O.J. Howard, who had seen the ball more often earlier in the season but had only caught four passes for 45 yards in the last five games. Against Michigan State, Howard caught three passes for 59 yards, including a 41-yard catch that set up an Adam Griffith field goal in the second quarter. But, Howard still had not had a touchdown reception all year. That would change suddenly in Alabama's upcoming battle with Clemson.

Kenyan Drake's 60 yards rushing on four carries also foreshadowed what would come against Clemson. Back and healthy after suffering a broken arm during the season, Drake would be ready for the Tigers.

Alabama offensive coordinator Lane Kiffin, fewer than two-and-a-half years removed from his infamous firing as the USC Trojans' head coach, had long ago been accepted and praised for his work with the Crimson Tide. His ability to adapt Alabama's offense to the changing college football landscape had contributed greatly to this championship run.

He met with reporters after the Cotton Bowl victory and assessed the Tide's remarkable offensive development from where it had started the season.

"Calvin Ridley had never played. Jake (Coker) had never played, and we had nine new starters on offense," he said. "So it was going to take time. We were still in a quarterback situation (early in the season), rotating guys and figuring that out. Luckily, we are a defensive team. When you are a defensive team, and can run the ball, it allows your skill guys and your quarterback to develop as the season progresses. But we knew at some time we would need these guys to play like they did today, and in the Florida game."

As Kiffin noted, Alabama was still a defensive team, and Michigan State found out the hard way.

Only once did the Spartans get past Alabama's 35-yard line, and it came late in the first half. With a first down at Bama's 12, trailing 10-0, but with a chance to go into the locker room with a score and some momentum, Cook made a huge mistake, throwing an interception near the goal line to the Tide's Cyrus Jones. It would be the Spartan's only real threat.

Asked about his "they're f..king everywhere" comments that thousands could see on the big screen hanging above the field, Cook confirmed them after the game, saying, "Yeah, credit goes to Alabama. Like I said before, leading up to the game you watch the film and the way their defensive line played, the way their linebackers filled the gaps, the way their secondary made plays in the pass game in the backend, everyone was aware how good of a defense they were. So yeah, I mean they were playing some good defense out there. The pass rush was there. Everything we saw on film was out there."

Still, Spartan fans, who outnumbered the Alabama faithful among the 82,812 people packing the sprawling stadium, did have that glimmer of hope even after Cook's crushing interception at the end of the first half. But Alabama's nine-play, 75-yard opening drive, capped by the first of those two Ridley touchdown receptions, made it obvious the Spartans were done. Up 17-0, and with Alabama's defense continuing to harass Cook and his offense, Cyrus Jones ran a punt back 57 yards for a score, and the lead was quickly 24-0. The game was over, although the final score would only get worse for Michigan State.

Alabama, meanwhile, had finally shaken off a year's worth of regrets over the way the 2014 season had ended with the playoff semifinal loss to Ohio State. There was no bowl atmosphere this time around, just business.

"I'm really, really proud of this team and our players," Saban said. "The focus for this game was completely different than we've ever had before, and I think it paid off for them. And we're looking forward to try and do the same thing for the next game."

CHAPTER SIXTEEN

Champions Again—
A Game for the Ages/Alabama vs.
Clemson

College Football Playoff

National Championship Game

Alabama 45, Clemson 40

January 11, 2016

University of Phoenix Stadium/Glendale, Arizona

IT HAD NOT ALWAYS BEEN this way. This national stage.

When Nick Saban arrived in Tuscaloosa in 2007, Alabama had not won or even competed for a national championship since 1992—15 long years for a proud program, but one mired in the past, suffering through NCAA sanctions, and miserably confined to mostly minor bowls.

Damion Square, a defensive end who was part of Saban's legendary 2008 signing class at Alabama, summed it up well back in 2013: "When I got there, we kept hearing that they (Alabama) had won 12 national championships. But in my mind, I'm thinking that the last one was in 1992. That's a long time. They had so much pride about that title game in 1992. But I'm thinking we've got to get something new around here."

Square, now with the San Diego Chargers, and that 2008 class—including future NFL players Julio Jones, Mark Ingram, Dont'a Hightower, Marcell Dareus, Mark Barron, and Courtney Upshaw, among others—jump-started a dynasty that included three Bowl Championship Series national titles and two SEC titles. By the time Square, a fifth-year senior, left for the NFL, he and his teammates had won 61 games in five years, a national record, and firmly established Alabama as the team to beat in college football.

Since then, the Crimson Tide had added two more SEC titles and was once again back in the familiar spotlight of a national championship battle on the game's biggest stage. Only this was different. This was only the second-ever College Football Playoff national championship game, and the first time Alabama had been in it after the semifinal loss to Ohio State a year earlier.

Only the Buckeyes and their 2015 championship game opponent, Oregon, had ever played what amounted to two bowl games back-to-back for a title in college football. Now it was Alabama's and Clemson's turn. They would not disappoint in a game for the ages at University of Phoenix Stadium in Glendale, Arizona.

By now, Alabama had spent the better part of a decade back as America's dominant team, even though this particular year the doubters were everywhere. Some of them, most notably Danny Kanell and Joey Galloway, were front and center nationally as the featured analysts on *ESPN*'s in-studio shows, including the popular *College Football Final*.

The questions had continued, despite Alabama's dominant victories over quality SEC teams after the Ole Miss loss. The Tide's rout over Michigan State quieted much of it, but there were still plenty of naysayers. The Spartans, with their pro-style offense, played to Alabama's defensive strengths. Clemson, with its fast, high-powered, spread offense, led by the best quarterback in the nation, would be able to handle the Crimson Tide, or so the thinking went.

"There was still a crowd of people who just wouldn't believe that Alabama was the best team in the nation," said Paul Finebaum, host of *ESPN* and *The SEC Network*'s *The Paul Finebaum Show*. "You know, the Danny Kanells and the Joey Galloways. Down to the final game, they all jumped in on Clemson. It's not always about Alabama with commentators. It's also about Alabama fans, and I think they (analysts) get sick of hearing from Alabama fans, and tend to go wishful thinking, picking against Alabama."

While many of the analysts were picking Clemson, the odds-makers in Las Vegas were not. Alabama opened as a 7-point favorite. That did not sit well with Clemson players and their coaches. After all, Clemson was the No. 1 team in America, with a record of 14-0 and riding a 17-game winning streak, the longest in the nation.

"Well, I mean, the message there is just, you know, we may not be the favorite, but we don't see ourselves as an underdog," Tigers coach Dabo Swinney said two days before the championship game. "We think that we've got a great team, and I think that our guys have done a great job of embracing every role that we've been put in for the last seven years, to be honest with you. That's why we've been so consistent."

On the surface, Swinney's steady, calm answer about the underdog role was hardly newsworthy. But he pointed out that his team's consistency over a period of years was no accident. The Tigers were here now, ready to play for the program's first national title since 1981, but there was still *that* word—"Clemsoning"—that over the years had come to describe a good team that manages to regularly lose to a lesser opponent.

Getting to Glendale and a date with Alabama had answered even Clemson's most ardent critics. But memories were still fresh from a couple of incidents in which writers had mentioned the word in news conferences, most recently after the Oklahoma game, when a reporter asked Tigers linebacker Ben Boulware, "Can we put Clemsoning to rest now?" Swinney stepped in immediately, saying, "Next question. Next question."

Swinney had already made it clear that the word was insulting and off limits during a heated news conference back in October, after the Tigers' victory over Georgia Tech.

"I think it's ridiculous that you're even asking me that question," a visibly infuriated Swinney told a reporter. "And that you even say the word. I mean I'm serious. I'm sick of it. I don't know why we even bring up the dadgum word. How about some of these other teams out there that lose to unranked opponents all the time? That's our 33rd win versus an unranked opponent. We ain't lost to anybody unranked since 2011, but I have to come to a press conference in 2015 and get asked that question. And that's all media bullcrap. I can tell you how they (Clemson players) feel about it. They don't like it. It's a lack of respect. It's not doing your homework and paying attention to what reality is."

Swinney wasn't done.

"Should not be asked that question. Period. That's how we feel about it. This football team right here," he said, his voice at Nick Saban decibels. "This football team right here has earned the respect. Ain't nobody given us anything. Not one ounce of anything. They've earned everything they've got. And when I have to turn on TV and people bring up that word, and they try to casually throw the word out there like you do, but it's still the word. And it shouldn't even be in the conversation."

Now, having shattered the stereotype with an undefeated season, an ACC championship, and a blowout Orange Bowl victory over Oklahoma, one of the nation's hottest teams at the end of the season, Clemson was unquestionably an elite team. The Tigers had more than earned their No. 1 ranking. But some wounds would not go away. Clemson and their head coach would simply use this as motivation.

No matter any real or perceived insults in media coverage, it was evident there was a mutual respect between the two national championship contenders. Even Alabama fans found it hard to work up a good dislike for Dabo Swinney, and there was good reason for it. Swinney was a former Alabama receiver and special teams player who had been a member of that 1992 national championship team, the one that destroyed undefeated and favored Miami, 34-13, in the Sugar Bowl.

But Swinney wasn't just any player. He had to earn his way. A native of Pelham, Alabama, Swinney joined the Crimson Tide as a walk-on, later received a scholarship, and lettered three years in a row. He became the first person in his family to graduate from college, got an M.B.A. in Tuscaloosa, then served as an assistant coach for the Crimson Tide's Gene Stallings.

Such deep ties made the upcoming contest difficult for some of Swinney's former teammates and friends in Alabama. Asked what he had heard from them, Swinney deftly answered, "A lot of them are just saying, well, 'Good luck to you,' or they're saying, 'Hey, I'm pulling for you. You're my brother, you're my relationship. But don't tell anybody.' So I've had a little bit of everything, but it's fun. There will be a lot of people happy one way or another Monday night."

Still, Swinney, added: "You know, to be able to be in my first National Championship and beat the University of Alabama, where I won a National Championship, would be pretty special."

The mutual admiration extended to the players, including the teams' two biggest stars, Clemson's Deshaun Watson and Alabama's Derrick Henry.

"We spent a lot of time together in New York at the Heisman ceremony," Henry said. "Deshaun is a really good person. I could see the motivation that he carries with him to be a good person. He works hard at both being a good athlete as well as a good person. I gained a lot of respect for him."

But now there was a game to play and a trophy to be awarded.

The stakes were high, as Clemson, the higher seed in their home orange, and Alabama, in visiting whites, took the field on a magical night in Arizona. *ESPN* and *ABC* play-by-play announcer Chris Fowler set the tone, and the stakes, at least for Alabama: "Nick Saban told his team, 'You deserve to be here, but you're entitled to nothing.' Anything less than a victory tonight and this season ends in disappointment for Bama."

Both Clemson and Alabama had won their semifinal matchups in blowouts, but this would be a titanic, dazzling battle that would go back and forth until one team, the Crimson Tide, took one of the gutsiest risks ever in a championship game—a stunningly successful onside kick in the fourth quarter—and the other, the Tigers, ran out of time after fighting to the end. When it was over, Alabama's 45-40 victory would earn the program its fourth national championship in seven years—a dynasty by any measure—and Nick Saban his fifth national title, putting him squarely in the sights of Paul "Bear" Bryant's record six championships.

This was, indeed, a game for the ages, one that delivered from almost the very beginning. Midway through the first quarter, Alabama's Alphonse Taylor, Dominick Jackson, and O.J. Howard opened a hole so massive on the right side of the line that Henry looked like the proverbial Mack truck rushing through it on his way to a 50-yard touchdown. It was the first big play in a game of big plays.

Howard, the big tight end who had been used sparingly as a receiver up until the Michigan State game, would do far more than block on this night. In the third quarter, he caught his first touchdown pass of the season, taking advantage of blown coverage by Clemson for a 53-yard score down the sideline. He added another spectacular score in the fourth quarter, again running past Clemson's coverage, splitting the field, and catching a perfectly thrown pass from Jake Coker for 51 yards and a touchdown. Howard would be named the game's most valuable offensive player, with 208 receiving yards and two touchdowns on just five catches.

Even Saban acknowledged after the game that Howard, with such enormous talent, should have had more touches in earlier games.

"Well, O.J., quite honestly, should have been more involved all year long," Saban said. "Sometimes he was open and we didn't get him the ball, but I think the last two games have been breakout games for him in terms of what he is capable of, and what he can do. I would say that it's bad coaching on my part that he didn't have the opportunity to do that all year long, because he really is a good athlete, and he's improved tremendously as a player this year."

A week later, Howard, a junior eligible to declare for the NFL draft, rewarded his coach's support by agreeing to return for his senior year at Alabama.

For now, next season could wait. It was time for celebration.

"This is what we stood up and said at the beginning of the season. We wanted to come out and win a national championship this season, and our team fought hard for that," Howard said. "And I'm just so proud of our team, and no team deserved this more than we do."

Henry also had another big night, rushing for 158 yards and three touchdowns on 36 carries. It was his tenth 100-plus-yards rushing game of the season and left him with 2,219 total yards and 28 touchdowns rushing, both Alabama and SEC records. It also marked his 20th consecutive game with a touchdown, the longest streak in the nation.

But the touchdowns from both Henry and Howard, and an exemplary second half from Coker (who threw for a career-high 335 yards and two touchdowns), were still not enough, together, to put away Clemson. It took a full team effort in all three phases of the game: offense, defense, and special teams. Especially with a nearly superhuman performance on the field from Clemson's Deshaun Watson, a dual-threat quarterback who threw for 405 yards and four touchdowns, and rushed for 73 more yards against the nation's best defense.

Watson did everything he could in a masterful performance, buying himself time against Alabama's rush and making plenty of pinpoint throws. But in the end, he said he could have done more.

"Going into this game, I was expecting to win," he said. "I thought we should have won. But like coach Swinney said, there were a few plays that we didn't really capitalize on, and I missed some throws. We dropped some balls and just had some miscues. Just some little things like that is going to really force yourself into a hole, and it's hard to beat a team like Alabama if you make those mistakes."

There was nothing Watson personally could have done to stop what became the turning point in the game, with 10:34 left in the fourth quarter.

Alabama had just tied the game at 24-24 with a 33-yard Adam Griffith field goal. Griffith and his teammates lined up for what appeared to be a normal kickoff. Clemson's front line pinched over closer to one side of the field, anticipating that Griffith would kick it deep toward the corner as he had routinely done. The Tigers' formation left an opening on the other side of the field, a formation Alabama had seen earlier in the game and had also studied on Clemson game films.

Alabama had practiced for this moment.

With the go-ahead from Saban, Griffith executed a pop kick perfectly into the open space 15 yards downfield on the far side, and the Crimson Tide's Marlon Humphrey ran under it, catching it at midfield. The onside kick had completely caught Clemson by surprise and even elicited a rare grin from Saban on the sideline. The "Tide," quite literally, had just turned in the game.

Two plays later, Coker found Howard wide open down the middle of the field for that 51-yard touchdown, and Alabama had a lead at 31-24 that it would never relinquish, though there was plenty of scoring yet to come.

"That onside kick was a big momentum swing for our team," Howard said. "It got the sidelined energized. Everybody was pumped up, and we went down and scored on the next drive."

The gutsy call by Saban endeared him even more to a team that already would run through walls for him, and it underscored a major point: that even with as much success as Saban has had, he was willing to do something no one expected from him to get the edge in a tight game. Of course, it wasn't luck. His team, as always, had meticulously prepared. Part of the process.

"I put my trust in coach Saban 100 percent," said Bama safety Eddie Jackson, who had a key second-quarter interception and was named the game's most valuable defensive player. "I wouldn't want to be no other place and play for no other coach than coach Saban. He's a great coach, he's a great mentor, and he always leads us in the right direction."

Saban said he pulled the trigger on the kick, knowing Alabama needed a lift and his defense needed a rest.

"I thought we had it in the game any time we wanted to do it," Saban said. "I made the decision to do it because the game was tied, 21-21 (actually 24-24), and we were tired on defense and weren't doing a great job of getting them stopped. And I felt like if we didn't change, do something, or take a chance to change the momentum of the game, that we wouldn't have a chance to win."

Swinney, who argued vehemently on the sideline even though the kick went 15 yards (only ten was necessary) and Alabama wasn't offside, gave credit where it was due after the game.

"It was a great kick," Swinney said. "First of all, he put it right in a good spot, and their kid did a great job of going and getting it. It was a huge play."

Ironically, Swinney and Clemson had used their own trickery, a successful fake punt, against Oklahoma in the Orange Bowl. But this was Alabama's night.

Still, it wasn't over.

Leading, 31-27, after a Clemson field goal with 7:47 left in the game, the Crimson Tide's Kenyan Drake took the kickoff, ran toward the opposite side of the field, and sped 95 yards for a touchdown, diving the last four yards into the pylon at the front corner of the end zone. An extra point extended Alabama's lead to 11 points at 38-27, and some breathing room.

But Watson and his offense came right back again, driving 75 yards for a score to cut it to 38-33, and a chance to steal the momentum. But once again, Howard stepped up with a huge play, this time taking a short pass from Coker behind the line of scrimmage, cutting around the corner, and running 63 yards for a first down at the Clemson 14-yard line. It took six more plays, including a clutch three-yard run from Coker for a first down, and Henry finally managed to score on a third and goal from the Tigers' 1.

The lead was now 45-33 with just over a minute left. Watson, however, still wasn't finished. He drove his team downfield, scoring on a 24-yard pass to tight end Jordan Leggett. But an onside kick, with just 12 seconds left, went out of bounds, caught by the Tide's ArDarius Stewart anyway, and an instant classic of a championship game was finally over.

"They (Clemson) were real strong. Never quit, either," Jake Coker said after the game. "I have a lot of respect for them after this game. They were real similar to us. Got a lot of fight in them. Great program. They just do things the right way. Either team could have won. It's just we happened to make more plays later on in the game."

Minutes after he and his team accepted the College Football Playoff National Championship Trophy, Saban reflected back on this team. Usually careful not to play favorites, the coach made it clear this championship and this team were different, in some fundamental way.

"I really wanted to do the best I could for this team, probably as much as any team I've ever coached, because I really did want them to have the opportunity to win this game," the coach said. "We didn't always play pretty in this game. It probably wasn't one of our best games when it comes down to flat execution. But when it comes to competing and making plays when we needed to make them, it was probably as good as it gets."

Saban should know. The man now has five national championship rings, four with Alabama. And the only coach who had more was a guy whose statue stands very near Saban's own on the Walk of Champions at the north entrance to Bryant-Denny Stadium in Tuscaloosa.

Asked about his standing in history, Saban said, "You know, I really haven't thought about it. After somebody asked me that question the other day, the first thing that came to mind was my first game at Michigan State when we played Nebraska, when Tom Osborne was the coach, and we got beat like 56-7. I had been in the NFL for four years and I'm saying, 'We may never win a game as a college coach.'

"And I remember running across the field and Tom Osborne—I think they won the national championship the year before and maybe that year, too—he said, 'You're not as bad as you think,' so that's the first thing that comes to my mind. So I learned a lesson that day, and you know, as long as you do this, it's always about your next play. It's always about the next game."

Soon enough, Saban would be thinking about that next game. Alabama would open its 2016 season against the USC Trojans in AT&T Stadium in Arlington, the same venue where the Crimson Tide defeated Wisconsin and Michigan State in 2015.

The upcoming season would mark Saban's tenth at Alabama, a bookend to a decade of big victories, lasting memories, and championships. And none bigger than the one in Glendale against the men in orange.

Next season, however, could wait. This was a night for celebration.

CHAPTER SEVENTEEN
A Decade of Excellence: Nick Saban's Alabama Legacy

NICK SABAN IS ENTERING HIS tenth season at Alabama, and with each passing year his critics have been reduced to a few scattered and lonely voices.

That's what winning five national championships—four at Alabama in the last seven years—will do for a 21st-century college football coach now being compared to perhaps the greatest of the 20th century, Paul "Bear" Bryant.

Saban accepted the Alabama job on January 3, 2007, after famously telling reporters he was not interested, that he wasn't leaving the NFL's Miami Dolphins. For a coach obsessed with doing things the right way, of remaining faithful to "the process," as he calls it, his public denials were a misstep, and he has expressed regret over them. But his insistence on making certain every detail is handled correctly, and his dogged pursuit of excellence, has produced an unprecedented run in modern college football, the kind that has shattered the record books and silenced much of the criticism.

It is hard to argue with the results: a 105-18 record at Alabama in nine seasons, all those championships, and a program that places strong emphasis on academic success in contrast to past eras. Above all, Saban has returned stability and prestige to a program that had devolved into chaos.

In the nine seasons before Saban's arrival, the Crimson Tide had run through a carousel of four head coaches, including one, Mike Price, who was hired and fired before ever coaching a game. The end result was a mediocre 63-48 record during those seasons, along with two separate NCAA investigations. The first, the most severe involving allegations that an Alabama booster paid a high school coach to steer a recruit to Tuscaloosa, led to sanctions that took away scholarships and bowl appearances. The second found that 201 students on 16 different Crimson Tide sports teams were involved in a scandal in which athletes obtained free textbooks for other students. The result was that Alabama had to vacate 16 of those hard-to-come-by wins before Saban's arrival, and five wins from his first year in 2007 (though Saban and his coaches had inherited the textbook scandal without knowing any football players were involved).

Saban's enormous success on the field has left his few remaining vocal critics looking petty and small, by comparison. And it's impossible to overestimate his influence academically. The football team's graduation rate has been among the highest of any of the Top 25 college football teams during Saban's tenure, even with so many of Saban's players opting early to the NFL draft after their junior seasons. (It bears mentioning that the Tide has been ranked in the *AP* Top 25 for 130 consecutive weeks, a school record, and the longest active streak in the nation.) When Alabama took the field in the national championship game against Clemson on January 11, 2016, 29 Crimson Tide players already had their undergraduate degrees, and three had earned their master's.

In Saban's world, self-discipline, making the right decisions, work ethic, and preparation extend as far into the classroom as they do on the practice field or in the stadium.

"We want these guys to succeed, first of all, as people . . . (to) be more successful in life for having been involved in the program," Saban said soon after the Crimson Tide defeated Clemson, 45-40. "We want them to all develop a career off the field, so that they graduate from school and have a better opportunity to be successful in life. We have one of the highest graduation rates in the country, and the best in our conference."

This was not the first time Saban has made that point—the *beyond football* point—and it wouldn't be the last. It's a message not lost on the parents of those five- and four-star recruits in high school: *send them to Alabama and your kid will get an education, in addition to playing at the highest level in college football.*

"We are trying to create value for players, so that they can have a better chance to be successful," Saban said. "That's always going to come first for me."

Saban has not only created that value for the players; the University of Alabama has benefitted from it, as well. The *New York Times*, in a November 5, 2015, story titled "Alabama is Rolling in Cash, with Tide Lifting All Boats," connected the dots between Saban's arrival and the university's skyrocketing growth in campus facilities, student enrollment, fundraising, and academic performance. During the last decade, "the success of Crimson Tide football can be measured off the field, as it has become a powerful engine for the university's economic and academic growth, a standout among other large public universities with a similar zest for capitalizing on their sports programs," wrote *Times* reporter Joe Drape. "Alabama's football pre-eminence on television and in the postseason, along with an aggressive plan to extend the university reach beyond the state, has helped attract a more academically-minded student body in the past decade from all over the country and served as the catalyst for more than $1.7 billion in fund-raising, according to those who have engineered the explosive growth."

Student enrollment at UA rose to 37,100 in the fall of 2015, 55 percent higher than when Saban arrived, and it is far more academically sound: More than one-third of the freshman class of 7,211 students (the largest in the school's history) scored 30 or higher on the ACT, putting them in the top five percent nationally. And more than half of the students now are from out-of-state, a stark contrast to the insular sort of recruiting efforts the university conducted in the past. The university's footprint has also expanded dramatically. Construction is omnipresent across its sprawling, tree-lined campus.

It would be misleading and inaccurate, however, to conclude that this is simply Saban's work. The university's expansion began soon after Dr. Robert Witt arrived as president in 2003. Witt, who later became chancellor of The University of Alabama System and will retire in the fall of 2016, began a massive capital campaign effort and directed a national recruiting effort for top academic high school seniors. But Witt also signed off on a deal to make Saban the highest paid coach in college football—a $32 million contract over eight years—when the Crimson Tide and then-Athletic Director Mal Moore hired Saban away from the Miami Dolphins in January 2007.

In a 2013 interview with *CBS's 60 Minutes*, Witt said, "Nick Saban's the best financial investment this university has ever made. We have made an investment that's been returned many-fold."

The numbers back up Witt's comments: Alabama's athletic revenues are among the highest in the nation, totaling $150.6

million in the latest report (measuring July 1, 2014, to June 30, 2015) released by the U.S. Department of Education, with a surplus of $30.1 million after expenses. In 2006, the year before Saban arrived at Alabama, the school's athletic revenues totaled $67.7 million with a surplus of $7.1 million, according to *USA Today*.

The investment in Saban, with the accompanying benefits of success evident throughout the Tuscaloosa campus, have not gone unnoticed in the nation's financial sector, well beyond the sports world. *Forbes* magazine, in its 2016 list of the world's top 50 greatest leaders, ranked Saban 11th.

"The dynasty was over. That was the consensus of the pundits after Alabama's 43–37 loss to Ole Miss in its third game of the season last September," a statement with Saban's listing in *Forbes* said. "The famed 'process' that Crimson Tide coach Nick Saban, 64, had used to win three national titles in football at Bama, while boosting graduation rates, and one at LSU had run its course, and the competition had caught up. Saban challenged his team: 'How are you going to respond?' When Alabama defeated Clemson 45–40 for another title on Jan. 11, 2016, he had his answer, and the dynasty—and Saban's legacy as a leader—remained intact."

If anyone questions why a college football coach is included in a list with such notables as Pope Francis, Apple CEO Tim Cook, U2's Bono, Amazon founder Jeff Bezos, and Supreme Court Justice Ruth Bader Ginsburg, chances are they have never been in a room with Saban.

"I've worked at *Forbes* now for 15 years, and interviewed plenty of big-shot CEOs and billionaires, and Saban's charisma is as strong, if not stronger, than most of the people that I've interviewed," said Monte Burke, who wrote a *Forbes* cover story about Saban called "The Most Powerful Coach in Sports" back in 2008, then followed that up with the first in-depth comprehensive biography of the coach in 2015.

Saban's charisma in one-on-one meetings, often a sharp contrast to his public persona of the hard-driven, always-fiery control freak, "plays a big part in his recruiting success," Burke said. "These high school kids are sitting there in their living rooms with their families waiting for this guy that they've heard about, that they've seen on TV, that maybe they've seen in a press conference where he's gone after some reporter, and he seems like the big bad wolf, and then he comes in and he's very businesslike, he's very charismatic. He's telling jokes. He's funny. He knows everything about these kids. One coach told me he knew what brand of chewing gum one of the recruits liked to chew."

Indeed, much of Saban's success on the field can be attributed to his legendary ability to out-recruit his rivals. Alabama signed another No. 1 recruiting class in February 2016, the sixth consecutive year the Crimson Tide has signed the nation's top class as determined by at least one of the media outlets who follow recruiting. Most of those classes have been a consensus choice at No. 1, beginning with what may have been the greatest single year's recruiting class ever—Saban's 2008 group, which including Julio Jones, Mark Ingram, Dont'a Hightower, Mark Barron, Courtney Upshaw, Marcell Dareus, Terrence Cody, Damion Square, Barrett Jones, and Robert Lester—all of whom made it to the NFL.

And as the NFL Draft approached in 2016, Saban was all but certain to increase his already-unmatched number of Crimson Tide players who have been drafted in the NFL in the past—48 in all— since 2009. Fourteen of those players were chosen in the first round. Many others have made NFL teams as undrafted free agents.

Those who serve as assistants to Saban understand just what a rare program he has built. It is a major reason Alabama offensive coordinator Lane Kiffin has given for choosing to stay in Tuscaloosa instead of pursuing another opportunity. Saban hired Kiffin after USC fired him as head coach during the 2013 season.

"I have a great job, and anytime there's any thinking different I just remind myself how many people would want to be the offensive coordinator for Nick Saban," Kiffin said four days before the Crimson Tide's playoff semifinal game with Michigan State. "He really took a chance on me. The phone wasn't ringing. At least for assistant coaching jobs, it wasn't two years ago. So I just felt like we didn't really finish what we started last year, and to see if we can go this year and finish how we should have finished last year. And get him another championship."

Although Saban has always been known as a defensive coach, his ability to open up Alabama's offense in an era of no-huddle, fast-paced attacks has underscored the coach's flexibility in changing with the times.

"I think that's something people don't give him very much credit for," Kiffin notes. "The thing about him is that he has always changed. They think maybe he's old school and it is how it is. It's not. Whether it's him bringing other people in, or sending us out to go see people. He does it on defense, too. He's always watching. He's always looking at a new approach to things. By him allowing us to do on offense what we do is a great example of that. At times this year going up-tempo, going fast. We don't huddle hardly ever. . . . He figured out, 'This is what's winning. Let's go see if we can adapt and use some of this.'"

Several times in recent years Alabama, known for defense, has simply had to outgun the other team in scoring shoot-outs, in games where the defenses struggled. The Tide's 45-40 national championship victory over Clemson is as good an example as any.

That win secured an almost-unprecedented fourth national college football title in seven years. Only Notre Dame, which topped the *Associated Press* college football polls four times in seven seasons during the 1940s, has accomplished the same feat. But that was in an era when the Irish didn't play in bowl games, college teams had shorter schedules, and there were no scholarship limits. Even the powerhouses of Miami in the 1980s, Nebraska in the 1990s, and Southern Cal in the early-to-mid-2000s, never won as many championships in as brief a period of time.

It was also Alabama's equally unprecedented 11th national championship since the poll era began in 1936, with Notre Dame and Ohio State tied for second with eight titles each, and Oklahoma and USC just behind with seven titles each.

Paul Finebaum, host of *The Paul Finebaum Show* on *ESPN Radio* and *The SEC Network*, had speculated before the Clemson game that if Saban won another title, the coach might just call it quits.

"I made a mistake of trying to think what I would do in his position," Finebaum said. "I'm not a gambler, but there's only so many times you can gamble on a masterpiece. He wins that game, he's declared the greatest coach of all time by some. I would have said, 'You know what? That's it, I'm going to TV. I'm going to the NFL.' But I think the confluence of success and age have affected him, where he now enjoys what he's doing."

Has the coach mellowed? It certainly wouldn't appear so when judged against Saban's more fiery news conferences. But Finebaum said he noticed a difference in the coach during a flight with him up to *ESPN*'s studios in Bristol, Connecticut, in the summer of 2015.

"He quizzed me on Birmingham," Finebaum recalled. "He said, 'What part of town do you live in?' When I told him, he said, 'Yeah, that's where my daughter lives.' I never heard questions like that from him before. Years earlier, when I was with him, you wouldn't know he had a son or daughter. Suddenly he's asking me about neighborhoods and all of this. So I think there's a big difference there."

As this past spring's Alabama practices proved, Saban isn't slowing down. But the coach said in a recent *ESPN.com* interview that others are beginning to use his age to recruit against him, a ploy that so far has not come close to working.

"I'm not looking to get out," Saban told *ESPN*'s Chris Low. "I'm really not, even though I know that's going to start being talked about now. What I have noticed is that it's the first time people are starting to say to recruits, 'He won't be there the whole time you're there,' because of my age. . . . My philosophy is that I'm going to be here for as long as I feel like I can be effective, impact the players, help them to be more successful in life, and continue to have a successful program."

That success has now rivaled that of the most legendary Alabama coach of all, Bear Bryant. Saban is just one national championship shy of Bryant's record of six. Bryant's titles, however, were spread over a 25-year tenure at Alabama. And two of those championships, in 1964 and 1973, were awarded by Top 25 poll voters before the coach and his teams lost bowl games. Saban's five titles, four at Alabama and one at LSU, have been won in championship games matching the No. 1 and No. 2 teams in the nation—and in an era of scholarship limits that Bryant didn't have to deal with until late in his career. Saban's teams have also had to get past what amounts to a play-in game, the SEC championship contest, to get to the national title, though his 2011 team was the exception. Alabama lost, 9-6, to No. 1 LSU during the regular season that year, then came back to rout the Tigers, 21-0, in the BCS national title game without having played in the SEC championship game.

There was no SEC title game during Bryant's era, and No. 1 and No. 2 teams were only rarely matched in bowl games at the end of the season. Yet, Bryant's accomplishments are legendary. The coach finished with a 323-85-17 record in 38 years as a head coach, a winning percentage of 78 percent, an astonishing achievement, considering Bryant coached over such a long period of time. His winning percentage during 25 years as Alabama's head coach was even higher, at .824, with a 232-46-9 record and 13 SEC titles.

Still, Saban's winning percentage at Alabama so far is higher than Bryant's, at .854. Overall, Saban has compiled a 196-60 coaching record (a .765 winning percentage) at Toledo, Michigan State, LSU, and Alabama.

Far from trying to distance himself from Bryant, Saban has embraced the coach's legacy.

"I don't think there's any question that there's probably only a few people in college athletics history that have had as great an impact. Maybe John Wooden at UCLA," Saban said on what would have been Bryant's 100th birthday in 2013. "I'm sure there are some other guys that have been able to be successful and sustain the consistency of performance in the program like coach Bryant did here. The effect that that had on the tradition and the institution itself and the fan base and just about everything."

Saban, like Bryant, has put a heavy emphasis on the means to the end—that doing things the right way is the first priority, and winning will follow.

"I think that as a coach, since I've been here, you can't have enough respect for the number of players who come back and talk about Coach Bryant, the influence and impact that he had on their life, and how he affected people in a really positive way, which is part of what we all try to do as coaches," Saban said. "I have probably as much respect for that part of what he did as anything."

At Alabama, there seems plenty of room for the legacies of both Bryant and Saban. At the Walk of Champions near the north entrance to Bryant-Denny Stadium, their bronze statues hold court, along with the other Bama coaches who have won national titles—Gene Stallings, Frank Thomas, and Wallace Wade.

But even for Saban, the shadow cast by Bryant may be too long to match, at least in terms of the often-intangible historical place in Alabama's long, storied football tradition. If not, one gets the feeling Saban is fine with that.

"Saban's a winner," said Finebaum. "He's the best recruiter I've ever seen, and he's possibly the best coach I've ever seen. But I feel like I can speak with some modicum of authority, having covered Bryant's end. Saban will never match Bryant as a cultural figure, as a larger-than-life figure. He's just not."

Despite the great differences in their eras of football, both Bryant and Saban have shared one great similarity, in addition to winning. They both came from rural backgrounds that played major roles in their ability to overcome adversity and achieve such a high level of success.

It is clear, for instance, that Saban's drive, even part of his process, comes from the coal-mining town of Monongah, West Virginia, where his father, Nick Saban Sr., owned a gas station and Dairy Queen, and coached the Black Diamonds, a Pop Warner football team, where Nick Jr. played quarterback. The elder Saban was a tough taskmaster.

"When it comes to motivations, and when it comes to influences, you can't discount the importance of his father," said *Forbes*'s Monte Burke. "His father was a very, very demanding person, a person who sought absolute perfection, or really what was impossible perfection."

Those demands were often manifested on the field, even when Nick Jr. threw touchdown passes. "When he came over to the sidelines (after a touchdown), instead of giving him a high five, his father would say that spiral was a little wobbly. He always found something," Burke said.

"To me that was one of the pillars of what is now known as Saban's process, which is sort of the breaking down of things into little bits that you can digest a little easier, and learning from the journey and not looking at the destination," Burke added. "I think to a certain degree, in order to adapt to his father's expectations of him he learned to love the process of doing it, and learned to find joy and happiness in that."

Saban has at various times recounted stories of his father's insistence on doing things the right way, whether it was ordering his son to rewash cars if there were any streaks left from the first wash, or mowing the lawn to perfection.

"When I was growing up, we had a reckoning every night when we sat down to eat dinner," Saban told one group recently. "And my dad sat there and pounded the table. 'Did you cut the grass like I told you to do? Did you put the mower away? Did you trim? Did you clean it? Did you rake?' And if you didn't do any of that, it was hell to pay. I don't care what part of it you didn't do. If you didn't do it right, you did it again."

Despite the unending demand for perfection, Nick Saban Sr., who died in 1973, would be "very proud" of his son now, Burke said. After all, that son has, to a large degree, carried the best of his father's lessons with him into the 21st century.

Saban's attention to detail was captured well in a 2013 *GQ* magazine story, written by former *New York Times* reporter Warren St. John.

"At Alabama, Saban obsesses over every aspect of preparation, from how the players dress at practice—no hats, earrings, or tank tops are allowed in the football facility—to how they hold their upper bodies when they run sprints," St. John wrote. "*'When you're running and you're exhausted you really want to bend over,' (Barrett) Jones says. 'They won't let you. You must resist the human need to bend over!'*"

Virtually all of Saban's former players, when asked, have said the same thing: that Tuesday and Wednesday practices during the season at Alabama were tougher than the games they faced on Saturdays. And no doubt, the players who will take the field in the 2016 version of the Crimson Tide face the same exhaustive preparation. And it's a safe bet that as long as Saban is in Tuscaloosa, the Crimson Tide will be a contender for conference and national titles.

Nevertheless, says Paul Finebaum, "The final obit on Saban, not to be fatalistic here, is going to be determined on when he leaves. I will tell you, had he retired on January 12th he would have gone down in my book as the greatest coach of all time, but let's say he loses in a semifinal this year to Urban Meyer and then never wins again, and Meyer wins three or four more. I've seen this in golf where everyone declared Tiger Woods the greatest golfer of all time. And then he hasn't won since. Now he can't make the cut. So Jack Nicklaus is back to the greatest."

Saban, clearly, is willing to take that chance. And part of it, as Finebaum pointed out, is that he continues to work well with young players.

"We watched Bryant grow old, even though he was just five years older than Saban is now when he died," Finebaum said. "And I think that's what stuck with people. He was like an old man. I don't think of Saban as an old man. Maybe because I'm getting closer to his age, I don't look at it like I did when I was 25 looking at Bryant. But Saban relates very well to young people. And I don't think Bryant did. Bryant was just kind of an old guy who did it his way. He changed, but I don't think he really understood the young players like Saban does."

CHAPTER EIGHTEEN
Looking Ahead: 2016

NICK SABAN STEPPED UP TO a podium on April 14, 2016, two days before Alabama's annual spring A-Day game, adjusted the microphone, and quickly scanned the room. He asked, as he always does, how everyone was doing, then wasted no time in reminding the gathering of Alabama football beat reporters that the man addressing them behind that podium was a guy who had been there a decade, despite the naysayers.

"So this is my tenth A-Day, and nobody here ever thought that I would be here for a tenth A-Day, if I could get you guys to tell the truth, which would probably be difficult," Saban said, almost breaking a smile and speaking slowly for emphasis. "But I do remember the first A-Day here."

That A-Day game in 2007, just over three months after Saban arrived in Tuscaloosa, drew more than 92,000 fans, at least 40,000 more than any previous Alabama spring game, and a national record that set off a game of one-upmanship among major college programs with their spring games.

"I think that probably did as much to establish the foundation and the spirit around here, to support players, make it special again for players to play here," Saban added. "Certainly it was special for Terry and I, who had been beat up a lot about coming here to start with. And it certainly did a lot to make us feel very welcome and at home, which ten years later we still feel very welcome, very at home, and very supported by a lot of people."

Given that Saban's tenure at Alabama has now been twice as long as any other stop in his head coaching career, one reporter, Marq Burnett of the *Atlanta Journal-Constitution* and *SEC Country*, asked the coach, "Did you expect to be here for ten A-Days?"

"Yes, God willing," Saban answered.

If anything, the tenth year seems to mark a turning point, perhaps, in dampening the annual rumors and questions about whether Saban will depart. There had been various reports over the years about both college and NFL teams trying to woo him away from Tuscaloosa, often with reports of huge amounts of money. The most credible of them included a serious overture from people connected to The University of Texas football program.

Saban has consistently said he was staying in Tuscaloosa, and only once before in his career, with that highly publicized departure from the Miami Dolphins to Alabama, had he done anything other than what he said.

Repeating remarks he had made earlier to *ESPN.com*'s Chris Low, Saban noted, "Everybody says in recruiting, 'Coach Saban's not going to be here.' They've been saying it for ten years now. So how long do you stay before that's not meaningful?"

Two days later, when 76,212 people showed up for the 2016 version of A-Day, Saban seemed about as content as he ever gets, watching (and coaching) in a blue blazer and red-striped tie as the Crimson team defeated the White team, 7-3. The far-from-flashy intrasquad game underscored the tremendous depth Alabama has on defense as it enters another fall season.

"It was really an outstanding day for me, personally," Saban said after the game. "We had a great crowd out there. I know our players certainly appreciate the support and passion that our fans have."

Many former players were in attendance, including the school's only two Heisman winners, Mark Ingram and Derrick Henry, both having reached the pinnacle for a college football player under Saban's tenure. Earlier in the day, the 2015 national championship team's permanent captains—Henry, quarterback Jake Coker, center Ryan Kelly, and linebacker Reggie Ragland—enshrined impressions of their hands and cleats into cement at the base of the university's iconic Denny Chimes tower on the Quad at the center of campus.

At Alabama, however, the talk was already turning to the fall of 2016, with the Crimson Tide opening against the USC Trojans at AT&T Stadium in Arlington, Texas, the same stadium where Bama had won two games, against Wisconsin and Michigan State, in 2015.

For the third consecutive year, the Tide found itself looking for a new starting quarterback. Going into the spring game, Cooper Bateman, a 6-foot-3, 220 pound junior from Murray, Utah, was No. 1 on the roster. Bateman had started one game, against Ole Miss, in 2015 before Coker, who had started the two previous games, took over and never relinquished the job. Others competing for the 2016 job included Blake Barnett, David Cornwell, and Jalen Hurts.

Hurts, a true freshman, had the best showing during the spring game, completing 11 of 15 throws for 120 yards and a touchdown. But, unlike Bateman, who had to compete against the first-team defense and its fierce pass rush, Hurts had faced the second team. Overall, the defense, which is almost a consensus pick to again be the nation's best in 2016, had 14 sacks.

"Sometimes when you match yourself against yourself, there's mismatches that you really can't overcome," Saban noted, and, though he didn't say it, the conclusion could be drawn that Alabama's defense is going to be a challenge for any team.

The coach also made it clear that the player combinations the A-Day crowd saw on the field on that bright April afternoon would not be the same as the ones the Crimson Tide ultimately settles on during the fall.

"I'm not sure we have all the best players on the best teams," Saban said. "There's a lot of competition in the offensive line. There's a lot of competition at quarterback. There's competition on defense in several positions. There are several players that are missing that didn't go through spring practice that will have a huge impact not only in how they play their position, but the leadership they show. So I don't think any conclusions can be drawn about anything."

It was all still months away from when conclusions would begin to be drawn. No matter; with an offense expected to include perhaps the strongest group of receivers in the nation— Calvin Ridley, ArDarius Stewart, O.J. Howard, and Robert Foster—and a defense in which every starter will likely play in the NFL, including Tim Williams, Jonathan Allen, Da'Shawn Hand, Reuben Foster, Ryan Anderson, Eddie Jackson, Minkah Fitzpatrick, Ronnie Harrison, and Marlon Humphrey, it was obvious the Crimson Tide will be ranked at or near the top of college football polls as the 2016 season begins.

Already, there were battle lines being drawn.

USC standout wide receiver JuJu Smith-Schuster, just after finishing his own team's spring game the same day as Alabama's, told the *Pac-12 Network*: "You know, Alabama's a great team, and

I think my guys are going to be ready when it comes to September 3rd. Our preparation is going to get us where we need to be at, and we're just going to make history."

Alabama, of course, would have a lot to say about that history. In due time.

Postscript

EXPECTATIONS HAVE BEEN SKY HIGH among Alabama football fans since Nick Saban's arrival as head coach in 2007. Saban and his Crimson Tide teams have more than delivered, with four national titles and a dynasty that—judging by yet another national No. 1 recruiting class in February 2016—might not be anywhere near finished.

These lofty expectations have extended beyond Tuscaloosa, and into the NFL, where Alabama has become known as a pre-eminent pipeline into pro football. No other team has produced as many NFL first-rounders or draft picks as has Saban and his program over the past few years.

So it was particularly disappointing on the night of April 28, when the NFL began the first round of the 2016 draft in Chicago, that three highly-touted Alabama players on hand—linebacker Reggie Ragland and defensive linemen A'Shawn Robinson and Jarran Reed—stayed in the green room, never hearing their names called. Only Alabama center Ryan Kelly, who chose not to attend, was drafted in the first round, selected by the Indianapolis Colts as the 18th overall pick. He became Alabama's 18th first-rounder in the Saban era.

The draft was very similar to the 2015 version, when just one Alabama player, Amari Cooper, had been selected in the first round, and seven Crimson Tide players were drafted overall. (Seven would also be selected before the 2016 draft was over.) But expectations can turn a strong draft into disappointment, even if the events of that first night faded quickly as spring turned into summer and fans began anticipating another possible national championship run.

The news, of course, was all good for Kelly, who had won the Rimington Trophy as college football's best center and got the draft call at his family's home in Cincinnati.

"I wanted to be around people that helped me get to where I am now," Kelly said during a news conference in Indianapolis a day later. "Obviously, going to Chicago you can't really bring 20, 30 people with you. It made it a little bit more home for me, having people with me, kind of sharing that experience with them. . . . It was a fun night. It's only going to happen once, so I tried to take advantage of it the best I can."

As euphoric as it was for Kelly, the wait to hear their names called was not easy for Robinson, Ragland, and Reed. But none complained, using it instead as motivation for later, and all three were drafted in the second round, along with Heisman Trophy winner Derrick Henry and cornerback Cyrus Jones.

Running back Kenyan Drake was selected by the Miami Dolphins in the third round, the No. 73 overall pick, and the seventh and final Alabama player taken in the 2016 draft. Within days, another eight Alabama players signed free agency contracts, bringing to 54 the number of Crimson Tide players on NFL rosters as the summer began, the most of any college football program.

"I'm always excited to see our guys get drafted, and it's always an extra boost when they get drafted in the first round," Saban said during an SEC West coaches teleconference on May 5, and reported by *Al.com* and *247Sports*. "We were happy for Ryan Kelly. I would have loved to see some of our other guys get an opportunity to be first-round picks, but I really do think they need to focus on the opportunity they have now."

Saban had been in attendance in Chicago with Ragland, Robinson, and Reed the night of the first round, waiting with them, but also understanding, as a former NFL coach, that, despite evaluations, it's impossible to predict where most players will land in the draft.

"I think our players all made a good decision based on the information that we had," Saban said. "I'm talking about the juniors now and where they were projected. But this is what happens. A lot of these evaluations that juniors get, sometimes the teams don't know as much about them. As they find out more about them, and also the competition out there, there's a lot of defensive linemen this year, which probably affected our two guys. But I think they're all going to have great careers. That's what those players should focus on, not where they got drafted but having great careers in the future."

Saban added: "I think that being a second-round draft pick is a great opportunity. Some guys may be disappointed about that, but there are only 40 guys in the country that got picked before you. And I think the media creates a lot of this because they speculate on who's going to get drafted where, mock drafts. But they have very little input from the teams themselves in terms of what they're looking for. So I think a lot of it is speculation. Sometimes it comes to fruition. Sometimes it doesn't. I'm just really proud of the way all of our guys represented themselves, their family, and our program while they were here, and in the draft."

Only Robinson and Henry, among the juniors on Alabama's team, opted to leave early for the draft. Standouts, including tight end O.J. Howard, inside linebacker Reuben Foster, safety Eddie Jackson, defensive lineman Jonathan Allen, and outside linebackers Tim Williams and Ryan Anderson, all chose to return. Their decisions are among the reasons the Crimson Tide is expected to be at or near the top of the preseason college football rankings again.

One thing seemed certain after the draft: the coaches and general managers of NFL teams who selected Alabama players seemed thrilled with their choices.

The Seattle Seahawks traded up to get Jarran Reed in the second round, all the while keeping their fingers crossed that he'd still be there.

"We're just very excited to be able to get him straight up," Seahawks General Manager John Schneider said after choosing Reed as the 49th overall pick in the draft. "Just didn't see him making it that long."

At a Seahawks rookie mini camp in early May, Reed seemed more interested in talking about his opportunity to succeed in the NFL than his long wait during the draft. But the 6-foot-3, 310-pound defensive tackle patiently answered reporters' questions about his frustrating night in the NFL Draft green room, saying: "It's extra motivation, you know, but things happen. I'll just stay humble and stay focused. That's all I can do. I'm in a great spot. Got a great coach. A great organization. Great teammates, great facilities, so I can't be mad with this. It just made me more hungry. It made me feel like I need to go back and improve my game more and play better and play harder."

At a news conference during the camp, Seahawks coach Pete Carroll called Reed "a terrific football player" and added: "The best players in the country he's played against, and he's always dominated. So we know that's likely to happen if he looked good here. He moved well. He understands the game. He just has a way about him. I can see why he was such a leader at the Alabama program."

Reed, who signed a reported four-year, $4.9 million contract, including a $1.7 million signing bonus, was clearly focused at the mini camp.

"It's been all about business, just coming in and getting ready to work," he said. "I'm really used to hard work."

Asked about the pace, he said, it's "just up-tempo. It's basically head to head, it's tough, demanding . . . running to the ball. Everything's up-tempo."

The main difference in the Seahawks camp and an Alabama practice, Reed said, is "we've got music on the field. We ain't got music on the field at Alabama."

A'Shawn Robinson was selected as the No. 46 pick overall by Detroit, and it's likely the Lions got just as much of a second-round steal as the Seahawks did with Reed. Robinson was a defensive force with 133 career tackles, nine sacks, and 22 tackles-for-loss at Alabama. But he may be best known nationally for one play, when he leaped completely over LSU's center and blocked an extra point attempt during the Tide's 30-16 victory over the Tigers at Bryant-Denny Stadium on November 7, 2015. For a lineman standing 6-foot-4 and 312 pounds, the feat seemed almost unbelievable and continues to be a YouTube sensation.

"I was going to jump over the top," Robinson said after the game. "I came to coach the first time they kicked a field goal. I told him I was going to jump over the top, and so I just jumped over the top."

Saban, in a news conference the following Monday, said: "LSU guys kept getting lower and lower and lower to where they were almost cutting to the ground. I'm not saying there was anything illegal about that. I think he (Robinson) just decided that if that guy was going to be that low, I'm just going to pop over the top. It was a surprise to us."

Bama's Heisman Trophy winner Derrick Henry wasn't expected to be a first-round choice, with most NFL analysts rating him as the second-best running back in the draft, behind Ohio State's Ezekiel Elliott, who moved all the way up to No. 4 overall pick. The Tennessee Titans selected Henry in the second round, as the No. 45 choice. Still, Henry, at 6-foot-3, 247 pounds, clocked a 4.52-second 40-yard dash in the NFL Scouting Combine, and he is likely to be hell-bent on proving the critics wrong as soon as the 2016 NFL season gets going.

"Obviously, you want to go in the first round, but to play in the NFL has been my dream since I was a little kid," Henry said during a conference call with Titans beat reporters. "It is a blessing and a surreal moment, and I am so excited to be a part of the Titans organization. I am glad they picked me to make my dream come true."

Henry gives the Titans two Heisman winners in the same backfield. Quarterback Marcus Mariota won the trophy in 2014. Henry will share carries with veteran running back DeMarco Murray, whom the Titans signed after a trade with the Philadelphia Eagles in March.

"DeMarco is a great back and has had great success," Henry said. "I am just going to learn from him and compete every day to make each other better."

Crimson Tide linebacker Reggie Ragland, the team's defensive leader with 102 tackles his senior season, was drafted by the Buffalo Bills early in the second round, as the 41st overall pick. Ragland's draft stock may have dropped due to a report from the NFL Network that a medical examination showed he had an enlarged aorta, requiring annual monitoring, but nothing that should keep him from playing. The Bills were happy to get him.

Ragland is likely to "start right off the bat," Bills General Manager Doug Whaley told the NFL Network.

"We want anybody that comes in to play the Buffalo Bills to know that they're going to have to strap that chinstrap up a little higher, and they're going to know that they're going to be in a fight," Whaley said. "That's what he (Ragland) brings, physicality. Then you add to the fact that the defense he ran in college is very, very similar to the defense we're going to be running this year. That and the combination of him coming from a winning program. All those qualities just made us feel like this is the type of guy we wanted on our team."

Ragland will be playing for Buffalo head coach Rex Ryan and his brother, Rob Ryan, recently hired as the Bills' assistant head coach for defense.

"I always wanted to play for coach Ryan, the Ryans, actually, both of them," Ragland said at a news conference at the Bills' rookie mini camp. "I'm getting an opportunity to do that, so I'm real thankful and happy."

Alabama cornerback Cyrus Jones was drafted by the New England Patriots in the second round as the 60th pick overall. Reporting to the Patriots' mini camp in May, he was eager to get started.

"Just hearing my name called has been a dream of mine since I was a little kid, when I first picked up a football," Jones told reporters. "And just to know that my hard work paid off, and to have coach Belichick and Mr. (Robert) Kraft to see something in me and want to give me an opportunity to make this football team better means the world to me."

Just as excited to be joining an NFL club was Kenyan Drake, selected by the Miami Dolphins as the 73rd player drafted overall, and the sixth Alabama running back chosen in the first three rounds in the past six years. Often injured, but one of the Crimson Tide's most explosive players ever, Drake will bring breakaway speed and agility to the Dolphins backfield.

Drake's confidence was high as he arrived at the Dolphins' rookie mini camp.

"I feel like, in general, with my skill set, in my eyes, it allowed me to be the best back in the draft, and I want to continue to prove that through my NFL career," Drake said at a press conference, adding that his versatility allows him to line up at other positions, as well. "I don't have to necessarily just be in the backfield to make a play. I can be lined up out wide, in the special-teams game, and not necessarily just return the ball, but kickoff rundown, making a tackle on a kickoff."

Eight other Alabama players were undrafted but signed free agency contracts, including Jake Coker (Arizona Cardinals), Richard Mullaney (Houston Texans), Dillon Lee and D.J. Pettway (New Orleans Saints), Dominick Jackson and Geno Matias-Smith (Washington Redskins), Darren Lake (San Francisco 49ers), and Michael Nysewander (Kansas City Chiefs).

Coker, who would be battling Matt Barkley for the No. 3 quarterback spot on Arizona's roster, tweeted: "Thanks to everybody for all the support. I really appreciate it. I can't wait to chase another dream in Arizona."

Saban said he was "excited for all the 15 players that we have who have a chance to make NFL teams—seven guys were drafted in the first three rounds. I think it's a wonderful opportunity for them. And eight others who signed free-agent contracts, we're really hopeful and excited that they have an opportunity now."

In Indianapolis, Colts fans will be watching this season to see if the Crimson Tide's Ryan Kelly and veteran quarterback Andrew Luck can bond into the kind of successful center-quarterback pairing that Jeff Saturday and Peyton Manning had there for years.

"Those guys worked hand in hand; they made each other better," Kelly said at an April 29 news conference in Indianapolis. "They made the entire offense better. You look at the teams that have been really great at any level of football, they've had great offensive lines. I'm just here to do the best I can. I think the coaching staff has put a lot of trust in me. Obviously, they have done their homework. It's going to be a challenge. It's not going to be easy. Just like everything else in life, if you want something bad enough, you work for it."

As if to underscore the importance of the pairing, Kelly was assigned a locker next to Luck.

"He's been great," Luck told reporters in May. "He's smart, he's conscientious, he's tough. I think he's got a little ornery in him. He's a little bit mean, which is great. . . . he's gone out there and really been impressive in a couple days of team stuff."

But Luck joked, "I can't be too nice to the rookies yet."

Kelly, for his part, isn't worried about the relationship. He knows it will develop in time.

"I know this is a very quarterback-driven league, and I came from Alabama, where it's a very NFL pro-style type of offense," Kelly said. "So I worked with three different quarterbacks and they're all very different. To have those experiences has helped me along the way, in how to deal with different guys. As far as now, I'm just going to do whatever I can to contribute to the team as best I can and do my job."

A rocky off-season.

Back in Tuscaloosa, the news on May 17 that two returning Alabama players—All-SEC first team left tackle Cam Robinson and backup defensive back Hootie Jones—were arrested on drug and weapons charges in West Monroe, Louisiana, sent a chill throughout the Crimson Tide program. Robinson, in particular, faced the more serious charge of possession of a stolen handgun, a felony punishable by a year or more in jail. Police said the stolen handgun was found under Robinson's seat in a parked car the two men were in at a city park in the early morning hours. A potential first-round draft choice in 2017, Robinson's career plans were immediately thrown into doubt.

Saban, speaking to reporters at a charity golf tournament a day later in Hoover, Alabama, took a wait-and-see attitude. The coach, despite his well-earned reputation as a hard-driving taskmaster, has consistently argued that players should be given second chances if they accept responsibility and earn their way back on the roster.

"We're still gathering information about the circumstance and the situation, then we'll figure out whether there's something internally that we need to do that is appropriate relative to what the situation is," Saban said. "If we can change their behavior based on what we do, that would be the purpose of discipline. Discipline is not necessarily just punishment, which a lot of people view it that way. It's 'How do you change somebody's behavior so they have a better chance to be successful?' That's the way we've always done it. That's the way we try to do it. That's the way I'd like to do it with my own children. I think that's the way most parents would like to do it with their children."

Saban's cautious response to the arrest of two players who had no prior criminal history seemed vindicated when prosecutors in Louisiana announced on June 20 that they would not proceed with the case against Robinson and Jones, citing a lack of evidence. Further, Quachita (Louisiana) Parrish District Atttorney Jerry Jones told KNOE-TV: "I want to emphasize once again that the main reason I'm doing this is that I refuse to ruin the lives of two young men who have spent their adolescence and their teenage years working and sweating, while we were all at home in the air conditioning." Though Robinson and Jones would no longer face prosecution, it didn't mean that they would escape discipline from their coaches at Alabama. Nevertheless, it seemed both players would have an opportunity to restart their careers.

Also adding greatly to the off-season angst in Tuscaloosa was the sudden departure in late April of Crimson Tide defensive line coach Bo Davis for alleged recruiting violations. In a statement, Saban said simply: "Bo Davis has submitted his letter of resignation. We appreciate all the contributions he made to the program, and wish him and his family the very best in the future."

Davis had worked with Saban at LSU and the Miami Dolphins, and was in his second tenure at Alabama. The Crimson Tide announced on May 9 that Davis would be replaced by Karl Dunbar, a veteran NFL assistant coach. But, oddly enough, Davis's departure would be referenced a few weeks later by Michigan coach Jim Harbaugh in a brief, but very public, feud with Saban over satellite football camps.

It began on May 31 when Saban, addressing reporters at the SEC spring business meetings in Sandestin, Florida, strongly criticized satellite camps, calling them "bad for college football." He likened them to "the wild, wild, west," adding that they are ripe for misuse and recruiting violations while purporting to be for the good of young players who might not otherwise get to attend a camp. Unlike camps on campus, where they could be better controlled, Saban explained, there were plenty of questions about satellite camps.

"Anybody can have a camp now," Saban said. "They can use you to promote their camp because 'Ohio State's coming,' 'Alabama's coming,' you know, whoever else is coming. Somebody sponsors the camp. They pay them the money. What do they do with the money? And who makes sure the kid paid to go to the camp? This is the wild, wild west at its best, because there's been no specific guidelines relative to how we're controlling and managing this stuff. It's happening outside our normal evaluation window, which means we're taking time away from our players. Our players come back to school today. So we start working and making sure that our players are doing the right things, with our strength and conditioning coaches, with our academic people, with the limited number of meetings that we're allowed to have with them. We're not going to be there because we're going to be going someplace else to look at some other guy."

Saban continued, "And then who gets exposed on that? I go to a camp. I'm talking to some guy I don't know from Adam's house cat, and he's representing some kid because he put the camp on, and I'm in trouble for talking to this guy? And who even knows if the guy paid to go to the camp? Is the NCAA gonna do that? I mean, we do that at our camp. We have people responsible for that. They're called compliance folks. What kind of compliance is at these camps?"

Asked if the camps benefit kids, Saban said: "I don't know how much it benefits anybody, because of all the people that say, 'This is creating opportunities for kids.' This is all about recruiting. That's what it's about."

Saban never mentioned Harbaugh, the leading proponent of satellite camps nationally, but when asked said: "I'm not blaming Jim Harbaugh. I'm just saying it's bad for college football. Jim Harbaugh can do whatever he wants to do. I'm not saying anything bad about him. If he thinks that's what's best."

That didn't stop Harbaugh from firing back with a tweet later that same day: "'Amazing' to me—Alabama broke NCAA rules & now their HC is lecturing us on the possibility of rules being broken at camps. Truly 'amazing.'" His mention of Alabama breaking NCAA rules referred to Bo Davis's departure as the Tide's defensive line coach.

A few days later, at a satellite camp in Atlanta, Harbaugh was asked about the tweet.

"The issue was what I said it was," Harbaugh told reporters. "Somebody that had just recently broken rules and has that in their history is lecturing us coaches, us other coaches, about potentially violating rules. I just thought it was hypocritical. I thought it was a hypocritical act."

Saban responded to *ESPN:* "That's his business. I don't really care what he thinks or tweets. I say what I think is best for college football and say what I think is best for the players and the kids. As I said, it's not about him or anybody else."

Saban, above all, has advocated for a college football commissioner to handle these kinds of issues.

"There needs to be somebody who looks out for the game, not what's best for the Big Ten, not what's best for the SEC or what's best for (Michigan coach) Jim Harbaugh, but what's best for the game of college football," Saban said at the SEC meetings in Sandestin. "The integrity of the game, the coaches, the people that play. That's bigger than all this.

"That's what somebody should do," he said. "Who's doing that? I don't know, because right now everybody is politicking for their conference. There needs to be a college football commissioner."

Roy Higgins of the *Times-Picayune* and *NOLA.com* may have come up with the perfect candidate when he wrote: "There are many coaches who would nominate the 64-year-old Saban for the job, partly because they are tired of getting beat by him, but mostly because they know few coaches care about the game of college football more than him. It has been his life's work."

Saban, of course, isn't ready to listen to such talk. There is the matter of the 2016 football season, his tenth at The University of Alabama. It had been a tumultuous off-season. The first game with Southern Cal couldn't get here soon enough.

Alabama 2015 Roster

No.	Name	Pos.	Class	Ht.	Wt.	Exp.	Hometown/Previous School
93	Jonathan Allen	DL	Jr.	6-3	283	2L	Leesburg, Va./Stone Bridge
29	Blaine Anderson	DB	Jr.	5-10	170	SQ	Charlotte, N.C./Myers Park
18	Keaton Anderson	LB	Fr.	6-1	220	HS	Florence, Ala./Florence
22	Ryan Anderson	LB	Jr.	6-2	249	2L	Daphne, Ala./Daphne
28	Anthony Averett	DB	So.	6-0	180	1L	Woodbury, N.J./Woodbury
94	Dakota Ball	TE	Jr.	6-3	254	1L	Lindale, Ga./Pepperell
6	Blake Barnett	QB	Fr.	6-5	200	HS	Corona, Calif./Santiago
87	Parker Barrineau	WR	Sr.	6-0	184	2L	Northport, Ala./American Christian Academy
18	Cooper Bateman	QB	So.	6-3	220	1L	Murray, Utah/Cottonwood
1	Chris Black	WR	Jr.	6-0	192	2L	Jacksonville, Fla./First Coast
75	Bradley Bozeman	OL	So.	6-5	320	1L	Roanoke, Ala./Handley
48	Mekhi Brown	LB	Fr.	6-5	240	HS	Columbus, Ga./Carver
2	Tony Brown	DB	So.	6-0	195	1L	Beaumont, Texas/Ozen
38	Hunter Bryant	TE	So.	6-5	222	SQ	Roswell, Ga./Fellowship Christian School
27	Shawn Burgess-Becker	DB	Fr.	6-1	205	HS	Coconut Creek, Fla./Monarch

No.	Name	Pos.	Class	Ht.	Wt.	Exp.	Hometown/Previous School
43	Gussie Busch	LB	Fr.	5-11	205	RS	St. Louis, Mo./Priory
67	Joshua Casher	OL	Fr.	6-1	294	RS	Mobile, Ala./St. Paul's
4	Daylon Charlot	WR	Fr.	6-0	195	HS	Patterson, La./Patterson
5	Ronnie Clark	RB	Fr.	6-2	228	RS	Calera, Ala./Calera
14	Jake Coker	QB	Sr.	6-5	232	1L	Mobile, Ala./St. Paul's/ Florida State
12	David Cornwell	QB	Fr.	6-5	221	RS	Norman, Okla./Norman North
66	Lester Cotton	OL	Fr.	6-4	315	HS	Tuscaloosa, Ala./Central
39	Paden Crowder	LB	Sr.	6-3	208	SQ	Vestavia Hills, Ala./Vestavia Hills
48	David D'Amico	TE	Jr.	6-0	211	SQ	Birmingham, Ala./Vestavia Hills
62	Will Davis	OL	Jr.	6-5	315	SQ	Letohatchee, Ala./Fort Dale Academy
30	Denzel Devall	LB	Sr.	6-2	252	3L	Bastrop, La./Bastrop
17	Kenyan Drake	RB	Sr.	6-1	210	3L	Powder Springs, Ga./ Hillgrove
36	Johnny Dwight	TE/ DL	Fr.	6-3	300	RS	Rochelle, Ga./Wilcox County
43	Lawrence Erekosima	RB	So.	5-7	175	SQ	Simpsonville, S.C./Clinton
32	Rashaan Evans	LB	So.	6-3	225	1L	Auburn, Ala./Auburn
80	Raheem Falkins	WR	Jr.	6-4	210	2L	New Orleans, La./G.W. Carver
29	Minkah Fitzpatrick	DB	Fr.	6-1	195	HS	Old Bridge, N.J./St. Peter's Prep
83	Ty Flournoy-Smith	TE	Sr.	6-3	247	1L	Moultrie, Ga./Colquitt County/Georgia/Ga. Military
10	Reuben Foster	LB	Jr.	6-1	240	2L	Auburn, Ala./Auburn
8	Robert Foster	WR	So.	6-2	194	1L	Monaca, Pa./Central Valley
69	Joshua Frazier	DL	So.	6-4	315	1L	Springdale, Ark./Har-Ber
48	Bo Grant	DB	Jr.	6-2	195	SQ	Valley, Ala./Valley
58	Brandon Greene	TE/ OL	Jr.	6-5	300	2L	Ellenwood, Ga./Cedar Grove
99	Adam Griffith	PK	Jr.	5-10	192	2L	Calhoun, Ga./Calhoun
20	Shaun Dion Hamilton	LB	So.	6-0	229	1L	Montgomery, Ala./Carver
9	Da'Shawn Hand	DL	So.	6-4	273	1L	Woodbridge, Va./ Woodbridge

No.	Name	Pos.	Class	Ht.	Wt.	Exp.	Hometown/Previous School
58	Alex Harrelson	SN	Sr.	6-0	234	SQ	Vestavia Hills, Ala./Vestavia Hills
34	Damien Harris	RB	Fr.	5-11	205	HS	Brea, Ky./Madison Southern
86	Truett Harris	TE	Sr.	6-3	220	SQ	Brentwood, Tenn./Brentwood
15	Ronnie Harrison	DB	Fr.	6-3	218	HS	Tallahassee, Fla./FSU University School
63	J.C. Hassenauer	OL	So.	6-2	295	1L	Woodbury, Minn./East Ridge
2	Derrick Henry	RB	Jr.	6-3	242	2L	Yulee, Fla./Yulee
84	Hale Hentges	TE	Fr.	6-5	235	HS	Jefferson City, Mo./Helias
96	Stephen Hodge	DL	Sr.	6-2	254	SQ	Akron, Ala./Hale County
42	Keith Holcombe	LB	Fr.	6-4	223	RS	Tuscaloosa, Ala./Hillcrest
88	O.J. Howard	TE	Jr.	6-6	242	2L	Prattville, Ala./Autauga Academy
26	Marlon Humphrey	DB	Fr.	6-1	192	RS	Hoover, Ala./Hoover
76	Dominick Jackson	OL	Sr.	6-6	315	1L	Cupertino, Calif./Homestead/College of San Mateo
4	Eddie Jackson	DB	Jr.	6-0	194	2L	Lauderdale Lakes, Fla./Boyd Anderson
33	Anfernee Jennings	LB	Fr.	6-3	255	HS	Dadeville, Ala./Dadeville
89	Bernel Jones	LB	Sr.	6-2	248	SQ	Montgomery, Ala./Jefferson Davis
5	Cyrus Jones	DB	Sr.	5-10	196	3L	Baltimore, Md./Gilman
6	Hootie Jones	DB	So.	6-2	219	1L	Monroe, La./Neville
35	Walker Jones	LB	So.	6-2	240	1L	Germantown, Tenn./Evangelical Christian
70	Ryan Kelly	OL	Sr.	6-5	301	3L	West Chester, Ohio/Lakota West
56	Brandon Kennedy	OL	Fr.	6-3	290	HS	Wetumpka, Ala./Wetumpka
81	Derek Kief	WR	Fr.	6-4	198	RS	Cincinnati, Ohio/La Salle
78	Korren Kirven	OL	Jr.	6-4	300	2L	Lynchburg, Va./Brookville
95	Darren Lake	DL	Jr.	6-3	315	3L	York, Ala./Sumter Central
25	Dillon Lee	LB	Sr.	6-4	242	3L	Buford, Ga./Buford
51	Jake Long	DL	Jr.	5-9	226	SQ	Vestavia Hills, Ala./Vestavia Hills
68	Isaac Luatua	OL	Sr.	6-2	315	2L	La Mirada, Calif./La Mirada

No.	Name	Pos.	Class	Ht.	Wt.	Exp.	Hometown/Previous School
55	Cole Mazza	SN	Jr.	6-2	240	2L	Bakersfield, Calif./Liberty
40	Joshua McMillon	LB	Fr.	6-3	240	HS	Memphis, Tenn./Whitehaven
34	Christian Miller	LB	Fr.	6-4	213	RS	Columbia, S.C./Spring Valley
41	Trey Moon	DB	So.	6-0	190	SQ	Cullman, Ala./Cullman
60	Brandon Moore	OL	Sr.	6-0	251	SQ	Cincinnati, Ohio/Hills Christian Academy
11	Alec Morris	QB	Jr.	6-3	233	1L	Allen, Texas/Allen
16	Jamey Mosley	LB	Fr.	6-5	221	RS	Mobile, Ala./Theodore
82	Richard Mullaney	WR	Sr.	6-3	208	TR	Thousand Oaks, Calif./Thousand Oaks/Oregon St.
46	Michael Nysewander	TE	Sr.	6-1	237	1L	Hoover, Ala./Hoover
42	Jacob Parker	TE	So.	6-1	218	SQ	Meridianville, Ala./Westminster Christian
94	Daron Payne	DL	Fr.	6-2	315	HS	Birmingham, Ala./Shades Valley
25	Buddy Pell	RB	So.	5-11	194	1L	Mountain Brook, Ala./Mountain Brook
72	Richie Petitbon	OL	Fr.	6-4	315	HS	Annapolis, Md./Gonzaga
57	D.J. Pettway	DL	Sr.	6-3	270	2L	Pensacola, Fla./Catholic/E. Mississippi CC
71	Ross Pierschbacher	OL	Fr.	6-4	298	RS	Cedar Falls, Iowa/Cedar Falls
45	Cedric Powell	DB	So.	5-11	185	SQ	Birmingham, Ala./G.W. Carver
66	Chris Posa	OL	Jr.	6-4	281	SQ	Commerce, Mich./St. Mary's Prep
89	Armani Purifoye	WR	So.	6-0	195	SQ	Kingsland, Ga./Camden County
96	Gunnar Raborn	PK	So.	5-9	187	1L	Lafayette, La./St. Thomas More
19	Reggie Ragland	LB	Sr.	6-2	252	3L	Madison, Ala./Bob Jones
90	Jarran Reed	DL	Sr.	6-4	313	1L	Goldsboro, N.C./Goldsboro/Hargrave/E. Miss. CC
3	Calvin Ridley	WR	Fr.	6-1	188	HS	Coconut Creek, Fla./Monarch
86	A'Shawn Robinson	DL	Jr.	6-4	312	2L	Fort Worth, Texas/Arlington Heights
74	Cam Robinson	OL	So.	6-6	326	1L	Monroe, La./West Monroe

No.	Name	Pos.	Class	Ht.	Wt.	Exp.	Hometown/Previous School
9	Bo Scarbrough	RB	Fr.	6-2	240	HS	Northport, Ala./Tuscaloosa County
15	JK Scott	P	So.	6-5	198	1L	Denver, Colo./Mullen
11	Kendall Sheffield	DB	Fr.	6-0	185	HS	Missouri City, Texas/Fort Bend Marshall
7	Cam Sims	WR	So.	6-5	209	1L	Monroe, La./Ouachita Parish
24	Geno Smith	DB	Sr.	6-0	196	3L	Atlanta, Ga./St. Pius X
21	Maurice Smith	DB	Jr.	6-0	199	2L	Sugar Land, Texas/Fort Bend Dulles
91	O.J. Smith	DL	Fr.	6-2	308	RS	Bossier City, La./Airline
31	Nate Staskelunas	DB	Sr.	6-3	210	SQ	Greenville, N.C./Arendell Parrott Academy
13	ArDarius Stewart	WR	So.	6-1	204	1L	Fultondale, Ala./Fultondale
3	Bradley Sylve	DB	Sr.	6-0	180	3L	Port Sulphur, La./South Plaquemines
50	Alphonse Taylor	OL	Jr.	6-5	325	2L	Mobile, Ala./Davidson
17	Adonis Thomas	LB	Fr.	6-2	228	HS	Lawrenceville, Ga./Central Gwinnett
14	Deionte Thompson	WR/DB	Fr.	6-2	183	HS	Orange, Texas/West Orange-Stark
54	Dalvin Tomlinson	DL	Jr.	6-3	294	2L	McDonough, Ga./Henry County
44	Levi Wallace	DB	So.	6-0	172	SQ	Tucson, Ariz./Tucson
59	Dallas Warmack	OL	Fr.	6-2	297	HS	Atlanta, Ga./Mays
23	Jabriel Washington	DB	Sr.	5-11	182	3L	Jackson, Tenn./Trinity Christian Academy
82	Thayer Weaver	WR	So.	5-11	180	SQ	St. Louis, Mo./DeSmet
56	Tim Williams	LB	Jr.	6-4	230	2L	Baton Rouge, La./University Lab
77	Matt Womack	OL	Fr.	6-7	315	HS	Hernando, Miss./Magnolia Heights
35	Thomas Woods	WR	So.	5-6	165	SQ	Birmingham, Ala./Vestavia Hills

Source: University of Alabama Athletics

Alabama 2015 Season
–By the Numbers

Date	Opponent		Score	Record	SEC	Attendance
Sep 05, 2015	#20 Wisconsin	W	35-17	1-0	0-0	64,279
Sep 12, 2015	MIDDLE TENNESSEE	W	37-10	2-0	0-0	98,568
Sep 19, 2015	#15 OLE MISS	L	37-43	2-1	0-1	101,821
Sep 26, 2015	ULM	W	34-0	3-1	0-1	101,323
Oct 03, 2015	#8 Georgia	W	38-10	4-1	1-1	92,746
Oct 10, 2015	ARKANSAS	W	27-14	5-1	2-1	101,821
Oct 17, 2015	#9 Texas A&M	W	41-23	6-1	3-1	105,733
Oct 24, 2015	TENNESSEE	W	19-14	7-1	4-1	101,821
Nov 07, 2015	#4 LSU	W	30-16	8-1	5-1	101,821
Nov 14, 2015	#17 Mississippi State	W	31-6	9-1	6-1	62,435
Nov 21, 2015	CHARLESTON SOUTHERN	W	56-6	10-1	6-1	100,611
Nov 28, 2015	Auburn	W	29-13	11-1	7-1	87,451
Dec 05, 2015	#18 Florida	W	29-15	12-1	7-1	75,320
Dec 31, 2015	#3 Michigan State	W	38-0	13-1	7-1	82,812
Jan 11, 2016	#1 Clemson	W	45-40	14-1	7-1	75,765

Alabama 35 - Wisconsin 17

Sept. 5, 2015
Arlington, Texas

	WIS	UA
FIRST DOWNS	17	27
Rushing	2	12
Passing	12	14
Penalty	3	1
NET YARDS RUSHING	40	238
Rushing Attempts	21	37
Average Per Rush	1.9	6.4
Rushing Touchdowns	0	4
Yards Gained Rushing	64	274
Yards Lost Rushing	24	36
NET YARDS PASSING	228	264
Completions-Attempts-Int	26-39-1	22-29-0
Average Per Attempt	5.8	9.1
Average Per Completion	8.8	12.0
Passing Touchdowns	2	1
TOTAL OFFENSE YARDS	268	502
Total Offense Plays	60	66
Average Gain Per Play	4.5	7.6
Fumbles: Number-Lost	0-0	0-0
Penalties: Number-Yards	5-50	11-120
PUNTS-YARDS	7-260	4-147
Average Yards Per Punt	37.1	36.8
Net Yards Per Punt	33.6	33.0
Inside 20	3	0
50+ Yards	0	0
Touchbacks	0	0
Fair Catch	2	0
KICKOFFS-YARDS	4-256	6-390
Average Yards Per Kickoff	64.0	65.0
Net Yards Per Kickoff	49.0	42.7
Touchbacks	1	2

	WIS	UA
Punt Returns: Number-Yards-TD	2-15-0	4-25-0
Average Per Return	7.5	6.2
Kickoff Returns: Number-Yds-TD	4-84-0	3-35-0
Average Per Return	21.0	11.7
Interceptions: Number-Yds-TD	0-0-0	1-41-0
Fumble Returns: Number-Yds-TD	0-0-0	0-0-0
Miscellaneous Yards	0	0
Possession Time	28:55	31:05
1st Quarter	6:09	8:51
2nd Quarter	9:27	5:33
3rd Quarter	8:32	6:28
4th Quarter	4:47	10:13
Third-Down Conversions	6 of 14	4 of 11
Fourth-Down Conversions	0 of 0	1 of 1
Red-Zone Scores-Chances	3-4	2-2
Touchdowns	2-4	2-2
Field Goals	1-4	0-2
Sacks By: Number-Yards	3-26	3-24
PAT Kicks	2-2	5-5
Field Goals	1-2	0-2
Points Off Turnovers	0	0

Alabama 37 - Middle Tennessee 10

Sept. 12, 2015

Tuscaloosa, Alabama

	MT	UA
FIRST DOWNS	15	28
Rushing	3	13
Passing	11	13
Penalty	1	2
NET YARDS RUSHING	86	220
Rushing Attempts	31	39
Average Per Rush	2.8	5.6

	MT	UA
Rushing Touchdowns	0	3
Yards Gained Rushing	91	231
Yards Lost Rushing	5	11
NET YARDS PASSING	189	312
Completions-Attempts-Int	23-43-1	26-43-2
Average Per Attempt	4.4	7.3
Average Per Completion	8.2	12.0
Passing Touchdowns	1	2
TOTAL OFFENSE YARDS	275	532
Total Offense Plays	74	82
Average Gain Per Play	3.7	6.5
Fumbles: Number-Lost	3-3	0-0
Penalties: Number-Yards	8-67	5-40
PUNTS-YARDS	8-288	5-201
Average Yards Per Punt	36.0	40.2
Net Yards Per Punt	31.6	39.0
Inside 20	1	1
50+ Yards	0	0
Touchbacks	0	0
Fair Catch	3	2
KICKOFFS-YARDS	4-231	6-381
Average Yards Per Kickoff	57.8	63.5
Net Yards Per Kickoff	36.0	41.5
Touchbacks	0	2
Punt Returns: Number-Yards-TD	2-6-0	3-35-0
Average Per Return	3.0	11.7
Kickoff Returns: Number-Yds-TD	4-82-0	4-87-0
Average Per Return	20.5	21.8
Interceptions: Number-Yds-TD	2-77-0	1-0-0
Fumble Returns: Number-Yds-TD	0-0-0	0-0-0
Miscellaneous Yards	0	0
Possession Time	27:04	32:56
1st Quarter	8:55	6:05
2nd Quarter	8:02	6:58
3rd Quarter	6:23	8:37
4th Quarter	3:44	11:16

	MT	UA
Third-Down Conversions	6 of 19	4 of 13
Fourth-Down Conversions	1 of 1	2 of 3
Red-Zone Scores-Chances	2-3	4-6
Touchdowns	1-3	4-6
Field Goals	1-3	0-6
Sacks By: Number-Yards	0-0	0-0
PAT Kicks	1-1	5-5
Field Goals	1-2	0-2
Points Off Turnovers	7	14

Ole Miss 43 - Alabama 37

Sept. 19, 2015

Tuscaloosa, Alabama

	OM	UA
FIRST DOWNS	16	29
Rushing	6	11
Passing	8	14
Penalty	2	4
NET YARDS RUSHING	92	215
Rushing Attempts	32	42
Average Per Rush	2.9	5.1
Rushing Touchdowns	2	2
Yards Gained Rushing	112	230
Yards Lost Rushing	20	15
NET YARDS PASSING	341	288
Completions-Attempts-Int	18-33-0	32-58-3
Average Per Attempt	10.3	5.0
Average Per Completion	18.9	9.0
Passing Touchdowns	3	3
TOTAL OFFENSE YARDS	433	503
Total Offense Plays	65	100
Average Gain Per Play	6.7	5.0
Fumbles: Number-Lost	1-0	2-2

	OM	UA
Penalties: Number–Yards	8-57	4-36
PUNTS-YARDS	5-199	2-84
Average Yards Per Punt	39.8	42.0
Net Yards Per Punt	40.6	42.0
Inside 20	3	1
50+ Yards	0	0
Touchbacks	0	0
Fair Catch	1	0
KICKOFFS-YARDS	9-583	6-336
Average Yards Per Kickoff	64.8	56.0
Net Yards Per Kickoff	41.1	41.8
Touchbacks	5	1
Punt Returns: Number-Yards-TD	0-0-0	2--4-0
Average Per Return	0.0	-2.0
Kickoff Returns: Number-Yds-TD	3-60-0	4-88-0
Average Per Return	20.0	22.0
Interceptions: Number-Yds-TD	3-32-0	0-0-0
Fumble Returns: Number-Yds-TD	0-0-0	0-0-0
Miscellaneous Yards	0	0
Possession Time	24:34	35:26
1st Quarter	5:03	9:57
2nd Quarter	5:19	9:41
3rd Quarter	8:39	6:21
4th Quarter	5:33	9:27
Third-Down Conversions	4 of 14	11 of 20
Fourth-Down Conversions	1 of 2	1 of 4
Red-Zone Scores-Chances	4-4	6-6
Touchdowns	2-4	5-6
Field Goals	2-4	1-6
Sacks By: Number-Yards	1-8	2-12
PAT Kicks	4-4	4-4
Field Goals	3-3	1-1
Points Off Turnovers	24	0

Alabama 34 - Louisiana-Monroe 0

Sept. 26, 2015
Tuscaloosa, Alabama

	ULM	UA
FIRST DOWNS	10	17
Rushing	1	8
Passing	5	8
Penalty	4	1
NET YARDS RUSHING	9	137
Rushing Attempts	31	35
Average Per Rush	0.3	3.9
Rushing Touchdowns	0	1
Yards Gained Rushing	57	153
Yards Lost Rushing	48	16
NET YARDS PASSING	83	166
Completions-Attempts-Int	20-43-2	18-32-1
Average Per Attempt	1.9	5.2
Average Per Completion	4.2	9.2
Passing Touchdowns	0	3
TOTAL OFFENSE YARDS	92	303
Total Offense Plays	74	67
Average Gain Per Play	1.2	4.5
Fumbles: Number-Lost	0-0	0-0
Penalties: Number-Yards	10-90	7-72
PUNTS-YARDS	12-413	6-227
Average Yards Per Punt	34.4	37.8
Net Yards Per Punt	30.8	34.3
Inside 20	2	4
50+ Yards	0	1
Touchbacks	0	1
Fair Catch	2	2
KICKOFFS-YARDS	1-62	7-452
Average Yards Per Kickoff	62.0	64.6
Net Yards Per Kickoff	49.0	40.6
Touchbacks	0	4

	ULM	UA
Punt Returns: Number-Yards-TD	1-1-0	5-43-0
Average Per Return	1.0	8.6
Kickoff Returns: Number-Yds-TD	3-68-0	1-13-0
Average Per Return	22.7	13.0
Interceptions: Number-Yds-TD	1-12-0	2-28-0
Fumble Returns: Number-Yds-TD	0-0-0	0-0-0
Miscellaneous Yards	0	0
Possession Time	32:32	27:28
1st Quarter	5:55	9:05
2nd Quarter	8:49	6:11
3rd Quarter	8:18	6:42
4th Quarter	9:30	5:30
Third-Down Conversions	3 of 20	2 of 13
Fourth-Down Conversions	1 of 4	1 of 3
Red-Zone Scores-Chances	0-0	5-5
Touchdowns	0-0	4-5
Field Goals	0-0	1-5
Sacks By: Number-Yards	2-12	6-26
PAT Kicks	0-0	4-4
Field Goals	0-0	2-2
Points Off Turnovers	0	7

Alabama 38 - Georgia 10

Oct. 3, 2015
Athens, Georgia

	UA	UGA
FIRST DOWNS	15	12
Rushing	6	7
Passing	6	4
Penalty	3	1
NET YARDS RUSHING	189	193
Rushing Attempts	47	38
Average Per Rush	4.0	5.1

	UA	UGA
Rushing Touchdowns	2	1
Yards Gained Rushing	202	223
Yards Lost Rushing	13	30
NET YARDS PASSING	190	106
Completions-Attempts-Int	11-16-0	11-31-3
Average Per Attempt	11.9	3.4
Average Per Completion	17.3	9.6
Passing Touchdowns	1	0
TOTAL OFFENSE YARDS	379	299
Total Offense Plays	63	69
Average Gain Per Play	6.0	4.3
Fumbles: Number-Lost	2-2	4-1
Penalties: Number-Yards	7-39	8-82
PUNTS-YARDS	7-287	11-420
Average Yards Per Punt	41.0	38.2
Net Yards Per Punt	37.7	28.3
Inside 20	1	1
50+ Yards	2	2
Touchbacks	1	2
Fair Catch	1	2
KICKOFFS-YARDS	7-453	3-179
Average Yards Per Kickoff	64.7	59.7
Net Yards Per Kickoff	43.9	39.3
Touchbacks	3	0
Punt Returns: Number-Yards-TD	6-69-1	2-3-0
Average Per Return	11.5	1.5
Kickoff Returns: Number-Yds-TD	3-61-0	4-71-0
Average Per Return	20.3	17.8
Interceptions: Number-Yds-TD	3-79-1	0-0-0
Fumble Returns: Number-Yds-TD	0-0-0	0-0-0
Miscellaneous Yards	0	0
Possession Time	34:03	25:57
1st Quarter	7:35	7:25
2nd Quarter	7:05	7:55
3rd Quarter	8:15	6:45
4th Quarter	11:08	3:52

	UA	UGA
Third-Down Conversions	1 of 12	3 of 17
Fourth-Down Conversions	0 of 2	0 of 0
Red-Zone Scores-Chances	2-2	1-1
Touchdowns	1-2	0-1
Field Goals	1-2	1-1
Sacks By: Number-Yards	2-11	0-0
PAT Kicks	5-5	1-1
Field Goals	1-1	1-1

Alabama 27 - Arkansas 14

Oct. 10, 2015
Tuscaloosa, Alabama

	AR	UA
FIRST DOWNS	10	22
Rushing	1	12
Passing	8	8
Penalty	1	2
NET YARDS RUSHING	44	134
Rushing Attempts	25	46
Average Per Rush	1.8	2.9
Rushing Touchdowns	0	1
Yards Gained Rushing	62	167
Yards Lost Rushing	18	33
NET YARDS PASSING	176	262
Completions-Attempts-Int	15-32-1	24-33-2
Average Per Attempt	5.5	7.9
Average Per Completion	11.7	10.9
Passing Touchdowns	2	2
TOTAL OFFENSE YARDS	220	396
Total Offense Plays	57	79
Average Gain Per Play	3.9	5.0
Fumbles: Number-Lost	1-0	0-0
Penalties: Number-Yards	7-44	6-56
PUNTS-YARDS	10-402	5-226

	AR	UA
Average Yards Per Punt	40.2	45.2
Net Yards Per Punt	36.3	43.0
Inside 20	5	2
50+ Yards	0	2
Touchbacks	0	0
Fair Catch	7	2
KICKOFFS-YARDS	2-113	6-357
Average Yards Per Kickoff	56.5	59.5
Net Yards Per Kickoff	37.5	41.8
Touchbacks	0	3
Punt Returns: Number-Yards-TD	2-11-0	3-39-0
Average Per Return	5.5	13.0
Kickoff Returns: Number-Yds-TD	2-31-0	2-38-0
Average Per Return	15.5	19.0
Interceptions: Number-Yds-TD	2-18-0	1-20-0
Fumble Returns: Number-Yds-TD	0-0-0	0-0-0
Miscellaneous Yards	0	0
Possession Time	26:07	33:53
1st Quarter	3:54	11:06
2nd Quarter	9:00	6:00
3rd Quarter	8:01	6:59
4th Quarter	5:12	9:48
Third-Down Conversions	5 of 16	7 of 16
Fourth-Down Conversions	0 of 1	0 of 0
Red-Zone Scores-Chances	1-1	4-5
Touchdowns	1-1	2-5
Field Goals	0-1	2-5
Sacks By: Number-Yards	2-18	3-16
PAT Kicks	2-2	3-3
Field Goals	0-0	2-4
Points Off Turnovers	7	3

Alabama 41 - Texas A&M 23

Oct. 17, 2015
College Station, Texas

	UA	TAMU
FIRST DOWNS	17	16
Rushing	11	2
Passing	6	13
Penalty	0	1
NET YARDS RUSHING	258	32
Rushing Attempts	45	25
Average Per Rush	5.7	1.3
Rushing Touchdowns	2	0
Yards Gained Rushing	295	81
Yards Lost Rushing	37	49
NET YARDS PASSING	138	284
Completions-Attempts-Int	19-25-0	22-45-4
Average Per Attempt	5.5	6.3
Average Per Completion	7.3	12.9
Passing Touchdowns	0	1
TOTAL OFFENSE YARDS	396	316
Total Offense Plays	70	70
Average Gain Per Play	5.7	4.5
Fumbles: Number-Lost	2-1	2-0
Penalties: Number-Yards	7-60	1-5
PUNTS-YARDS	9-386	6-270
Average Yards Per Punt	42.9	45.0
Net Yards Per Punt	26.3	39.2
Inside 20	0	1
50+ Yards	4	1
Touchbacks	3	0
Fair Catch	0	2
KICKOFFS-YARDS	8-511	6-365
Average Yards Per Kickoff	63.9	60.8
Net Yards Per Kickoff	40.5	42.3
Touchbacks	5	2

	UA	TAMU
Punt Returns: Number-Yards-TD	3-35-0	5-89-1
Average Per Return	11.7	17.8
Kickoff Returns: Number-Yds-TD	4-61-0	3-62-0
Average Per Return	15.2	20.7
Interceptions: Number-Yds-TD	4-207-3	0-0-0
Fumble Returns: Number-Yds-TD	0-0-0	0-0-0
Miscellaneous Yards	0	0
Possession Time	36:22	23:38
1st Quarter	9:00	6:00
2nd Quarter	6:56	8:04
3rd Quarter	11:02	3:58
4th Quarter	9:24	5:36
Third-Down Conversions	4 of 16	7 of 18
Fourth-Down Conversions	1 of 1	0 of 1
Red-Zone Scores-Chances	3-4	2-2
Touchdowns	1-4	1-2
Field Goals	2-4	1-2
Sacks By: Number-Yards	6-34	1-6
PAT Kicks	5-5	2-2
Field Goals	2-2	3-5
Points Off Turnovers	24	7

Alabama 19 - Tennessee 14

Oct. 24, 2015
Tuscaloosa, Alabama

	TN	UA
FIRST DOWNS	21	23
Rushing	11	10
Passing	9	12
Penalty	1	1
NET YARDS RUSHING	132	117
Rushing Attempts	39	42
Average Per Rush	3.4	2.8

	TN	UA
Rushing Touchdowns	1	2
Yards Gained Rushing	172	162
Yards Lost Rushing	40	45
NET YARDS PASSING	171	247
Completions-Attempts-Int	13-22-0	21-27-1
Average Per Attempt	7.8	9.1
Average Per Completion	13.2	11.8
Passing Touchdowns	1	0
TOTAL OFFENSE YARDS	303	364
Total Offense Plays	61	69
Average Gain Per Play	5.0	5.3
Fumbles: Number-Lost	1-1	0-0
Penalties: Number-Yards	6-30	7-64
PUNTS-YARDS	4-173	4-199
Average Yards Per Punt	43.2	49.8
Net Yards Per Punt	43.2	44.0
Inside 20	0	2
50+ Yards	1	2
Touchbacks	0	1
Fair Catch	2	2
KICKOFFS-YARDS	3-195	5-323
Average Yards Per Kickoff	65.0	64.6
Net Yards Per Kickoff	36.0	38.4
Touchbacks	1	4
Punt Returns: Number-Yards-TD	1-3-0	0-0-0
Average Per Return	3.0	0.0
Kickoff Returns: Number-Yds-TD	1-31-0	2-62-0
Average Per Return	31.0	31.0
Interceptions: Number-Yds-TD	1-1-0	0-0-0
Fumble Returns: Number-Yds-TD	0-0-0	1-9-0
Miscellaneous Yards	0	0
Possession Time	24:21	35:39
1st Quarter	8:22	6:38
2nd Quarter	7:25	7:35
3rd Quarter	5:15	9:45
4th Quarter	3:19	11:41

	TN	UA
Third-Down Conversions	7 of 13	5 of 12
Fourth-Down Conversions	0 of 0	0 of 0
Red-Zone Scores-Chances	2-3	4-5
Touchdowns	2-3	2-5
Field Goals	0-3	2-5
Sacks By: Number-Yards	5-27	5-38
PAT Kicks	2-2	1-1
Field Goals	0-3	2-2
Points Off Turnovers	0	0

Alabama 30 - LSU 16

Nov. 7, 2015
Tuscaloosa, Alabama

	LS	UA
FIRST DOWNS	12	28
Rushing	3	14
Passing	5	12
Penalty	4	2
NET YARDS RUSHING	54	250
Rushing Attempts	26	55
Average Per Rush	2.1	4.5
Rushing Touchdowns	1	3
Yards Gained Rushing	77	290
Yards Lost Rushing	23	40
NET YARDS PASSING	128	184
Completions-Attempts-Int	6-19-1	18-24-0
Average Per Attempt	6.7	7.7
Average Per Completion	21.3	10.2
Passing Touchdowns	1	0
TOTAL OFFENSE YARDS	182	434
Total Offense Plays	45	79
Average Gain Per Play	4.0	5.5
Fumbles: Number-Lost	0-0	2-1

	LS	UA
Penalties: Number-Yards	7-48	9-88
PUNTS-YARDS	7-296	3-135
Average Yards Per Punt	42.3	45.0
Net Yards Per Punt	39.0	43.3
Inside 20	2	1
50+ Yards	1	1
Touchbacks	0	0
Fair Catch	3	0
KICKOFFS-YARDS	4-238	7-448
Average Yards Per Kickoff	59.5	64.0
Net Yards Per Kickoff	45.8	47.1
Touchbacks	0	3
Punt Returns: Number-Yards-TD	2-5-0	2-23-0
Average Per Return	2.5	11.5
Kickoff Returns: Number-Yds-TD	4-43-0	3-55-0
Average Per Return	10.8	18.3
Interceptions: Number-Yds-TD	0-0-0	1-4-0
Fumble Returns: Number-Yds-TD	0-0-0	0-0-0
Miscellaneous Yards	0	0
Possession Time	20:33	39:27
1st Quarter	6:21	8:39
2nd Quarter	5:21	9:39
3rd Quarter	6:03	8:57
4th Quarter	2:48	12:12
Third-Down Conversions	3 of 11	7 of 15
Fourth-Down Conversions	0 of 0	1 of 2
Red-Zone Scores-Chances	1-1	5-6
Touchdowns	1-1	3-6
Field Goals	0-1	2-6
Sacks By: Number-Yards	3-31	2-9
PAT Kicks	1-2	3-3
Field Goals	1-1	3-3
Points Off Turnovers	6	7

Alabama 31 - Mississippi State 6

Nov. 14, 2015
Starkville, Mississippi

	UA	MS
FIRST DOWNS	13	20
Rushing	8	8
Passing	4	11
Penalty	1	1
NET YARDS RUSHING	235	89
Rushing Attempts	30	42
Average Per Rush	7.8	2.1
Rushing Touchdowns	2	0
Yards Gained Rushing	239	149
Yards Lost Rushing	4	60
NET YARDS PASSING	144	304
Completions-Attempts-Int	15-25-1	23-45-1
Average Per Attempt	5.8	6.8
Average Per Completion	9.6	13.2
Passing Touchdowns	1	0
TOTAL OFFENSE YARDS	379	393
Total Offense Plays	55	87
Average Gain Per Play	6.9	4.5
Fumbles: Number-Lost	0-0	3-1
Penalties: Number-Yards	4-40	4-40
PUNTS-YARDS	5-200	6-266
Average Yards Per Punt	40.0	44.3
Net Yards Per Punt	39.4	29.5
Inside 20	1	2
50+ Yards	0	2
Touchbacks	0	1
Fair Catch	2	1
KICKOFFS-YARDS	6-377	3-192
Average Yards Per Kickoff	62.8	64.0
Net Yards Per Kickoff	45.0	47.3
Touchbacks	2	2

	UA	MS
Punt Returns: Number-Yards-TD	1-69-1	1-3-0
Average Per Return	69.0	3.0
Kickoff Returns: Number-Yds-TD	0-0-0	4-57-0
Average Per Return	0.0	14.2
Interceptions: Number-Yds-TD	1-29-0	1-0-0
Fumble Returns: Number-Yds-TD	0-0-0	0-0-0
Miscellaneous Yards	0	-20
Possession Time	26:30	33:30
1st Quarter	5:33	9:27
2nd Quarter	3:11	11:49
3rd Quarter	7:46	7:14
4th Quarter	10:00	5:00
Third-Down Conversions	5 of 14	7 of 19
Fourth-Down Conversions	0 of 1	1 of 4
Red-Zone Scores-Chances	0-2	2-3
Touchdowns	0-2	0-3
Field Goals	0-2	2-3
Sacks By: Number-Yards	9-55	0-0
PAT Kicks	4-4	0-0
Field Goals	1-2	2-3
Points Off Turnovers	0	0

Alabama 56 - Charleston Southern 6

Nov. 21, 2015
Tuscaloosa, Alabama

	CHSO	UA
FIRST DOWNS	8	23
Rushing	5	13
Passing	2	10
Penalty	1	0
NET YARDS RUSHING	85	195
Rushing Attempts	36	35
Average Per Rush	2.4	5.6

	CHSO	UA
Rushing Touchdowns	1	4
Yards Gained Rushing	110	201
Yards Lost Rushing	25	6
NET YARDS PASSING	49	208
Completions-Attempts-Int	5-10-1	19-25-0
Average Per Attempt	4.9	8.3
Average Per Completion	9.8	10.9
Passing Touchdowns	0	2
TOTAL OFFENSE YARDS	134	403
Total Offense Plays	46	60
Average Gain Per Play	2.9	6.7
Fumbles: Number-Lost	3-1	0-0
Penalties: Number-Yards	3-10	2-30
PUNTS-YARDS	8-277	0-0
Average Yards Per Punt	34.6	0.0
Net Yards Per Punt	19.2	0.0
Inside 20	2	0
50+ Yards	0	0
Touchbacks	0	0
Fair Catch	3	0
KICKOFFS-YARDS	2-75	9-576
Average Yards Per Kickoff	37.5	64.0
Net Yards Per Kickoff	27.0	44.0
Touchbacks	0	6
Punt Returns: Number-Yards-TD	0-0-0	3-123-2
Average Per Return	0.0	41.0
Kickoff Returns: Number-Yds-TD	2-30-0	2-21-0
Average Per Return	15.0	10.5
Interceptions: Number-Yds-TD	0-0-0	1-34-0
Fumble Returns: Number-Yds-TD	0-0-0	1-18-0
Miscellaneous Yards	0	0
Possession Time	31:18	28:42
1st Quarter	6:27	8:33
2nd Quarter	11:37	3:23
3rd Quarter	7:52	7:08
4th Quarter	5:22	9:38

	CHSO	UA
Third-Down Conversions	1 of 10	5 of 9
Fourth-Down Conversions	1 of 1	2 of 3
Red-Zone Scores-Chances	1-1	4-5
Touchdowns	1-1	4-5
Field Goals	0-1	0-5
Sacks By: Number-Yards	1-2	0-0
PAT Kicks	0-0	8-8
Field Goals	0-0	0-1
Points Off Turnovers	0	7

Alabama 29 - Auburn 13

Nov. 28, 2015
Auburn, Alabama

	UA	AU
FIRST DOWNS	24	12
Rushing	13	6
Passing	8	4
Penalty	3	2
NET YARDS RUSHING	286	91
Rushing Attempts	50	37
Average Per Rush	5.7	2.5
Rushing Touchdowns	1	0
Yards Gained Rushing	294	131
Yards Lost Rushing	8	40
NET YARDS PASSING	179	169
Completions-Attempts-Int	17-26-0	10-23-0
Average Per Attempt	6.9	7.3
Average Per Completion	10.5	16.9
Passing Touchdowns	1	1
TOTAL OFFENSE YARDS	465	260
Total Offense Plays	76	60
Average Gain Per Play	6.1	4.3
Fumbles: Number-Lost	0-0	2-1

	UA	AU
Penalties: Number-Yards	7-65	8-62
PUNTS-YARDS	3-145	5-202
Average Yards Per Punt	48.3	40.4
Net Yards Per Punt	28.0	39.8
Inside 20	0	3
50+ Yards	1	0
Touchbacks	2	0
Fair Catch	0	3
KICKOFFS-YARDS	8-520	4-260
Average Yards Per Kickoff	65.0	65.0
Net Yards Per Kickoff	39.9	42.5
Touchbacks	7	2
Punt Returns: Number-Yards-TD	1-3-0	1-21-0
Average Per Return	3.0	21.0
Kickoff Returns: Number-Yds-TD	2-40-0	1-26-0
Average Per Return	20.0	26.0
Interceptions: Number-Yds-TD	0-0-0	0-0-0
Fumble Returns: Number-Yds-TD	0-0-0	0-0-0
Miscellaneous Yards	0	0
Possession Time	35:23	24:37
1st Quarter	7:11	7:49
2nd Quarter	6:34	8:26
3rd Quarter	11:09	3:51
4th Quarter	10:29	4:31
Third-Down Conversions	5 of 16	3 of 15
Fourth-Down Conversions	1 of 2	1 of 2
Red-Zone Scores-Chances	2-2	1-1
Touchdowns	0-2	0-1
Field Goals	2-2	1-1
Sacks By: Number-Yards	3-32	0-0
PAT Kicks	2-2	1-1
Field Goals	5-5	2-3
Points Off Turnovers	0	0

Southeastern Conference Championship
Alabama 29 - Florida 15

Dec. 5, 2015
Atlanta, Georgia

	UF	UA
FIRST DOWNS	7	25
Rushing	1	14
Passing	6	9
Penalty	0	2
NET YARDS RUSHING	15	233
Rushing Attempts	21	58
Average Per Rush	0.7	4.0
Rushing Touchdowns	0	1
Yards Gained Rushing	57	260
Yards Lost Rushing	42	27
NET YARDS PASSING	165	204
Completions-Attempts-Int	9-24-1	18-26-0
Average Per Attempt	6.9	7.8
Average Per Completion	18.3	11.3
Passing Touchdowns	1	2
TOTAL OFFENSE YARDS	180	437
Total Offense Plays	45	84
Average Gain Per Play	4.0	5.2
Fumbles: Number-Lost	1-0	2-1
Penalties: Number-Yards	5-51	5-35
PUNTS-YARDS	9-414	6-307
Average Yards Per Punt	46.0	51.2
Net Yards Per Punt	41.0	37.2
Inside 20	1	5
50+ Yards	5	4
Touchbacks	0	0
Fair Catch	0	2
KICKOFFS-YARDS	4-213	6-390
Average Yards Per Kickoff	53.2	65.0

	UF	UA
Net Yards Per Kickoff	35.5	41.0
Touchbacks	1	4
Punt Returns: Number-Yards-TD	3-84-1	8-45-0
Average Per Return	28.0	5.6
Kickoff Returns: Number-Yds-TD	2-44-0	2-46-0
Average Per Return	22.0	23.0
Interceptions: Number-Yds-TD	0-0-0	1--1-0
Fumble Returns: Number-Yds-TD	0-0-0	0-0-0
Miscellaneous Yards	0	15
Possession Time	16:31	43:29
1st Quarter	6:35	8:25
2nd Quarter	5:13	9:47
3rd Quarter	1:05	13:55
4th Quarter	3:38	11:22
Third-Down Conversions	0 of 11	7 of 17
Fourth-Down Conversions	0 of 1	1 of 1
Red-Zone Scores-Chances	0-0	4-6
Touchdowns	0-0	2-6
Field Goals	0-0	2-6
Sacks By: Number-Yards	2-17	5-36
PAT Kicks	1-1	3-3
Field Goals	0-1	2-3
Points Off Turnovers	0	0

Cotton Bowl
Alabama 38 - Michigan State 0

Dec. 31, 2015
Arlington, Texas

	MSU	UA
FIRST DOWNS	16	21
Rushing	2	7
Passing	11	12
Penalty	3	2

	MSU	UA
NET YARDS RUSHING	29	154
Rushing Attempts	26	35
Average Per Rush	1.1	4.4
Rushing Touchdowns	0	2
Yards Gained Rushing	64	174
Yards Lost Rushing	35	20
NET YARDS PASSING	210	286
Completions-Attempts-Int	19-39-2	25-31-0
Average Per Attempt	5.4	9.2
Average Per Completion	11.1	11.4
Passing Touchdowns	0	2
TOTAL OFFENSE YARDS	239	440
Total Offense Plays	65	66
Average Gain Per Play	3.7	6.7
Fumbles: Number-Lost	2-0	2-0
Penalties: Number-Yards	6-33	6-69
PUNTS-YARDS	9-411	6-279
Average Yards Per Punt	45.7	46.5
Net Yards Per Punt	34.6	40.5
Inside 20	1	4
50+ Yards	2	3
Touchbacks	1	1
Fair Catch	2	0
KICKOFFS-YARDS	1-65	7-443
Average Yards Per Kickoff	65.0	63.3
Net Yards Per Kickoff	40.0	42.3
Touchbacks	1	5
Punt Returns: Number-Yards-TD	3-16-0	5-80-1
Average Per Return	5.3	16.0
Kickoff Returns: Number-Yds-TD	1-22-0	0-0-0
Average Per Return	22.0	0.0
Interceptions: Number-Yds-TD	0-0-0	2-21-0
Fumble Returns: Number-Yds-TD	0-0-0	0-0-0
Miscellaneous Yards	0	0
Possession Time	27:04	32:56
1st Quarter	7:56	7:04

	MSU	UA
2nd Quarter	5:26	9:34
3rd Quarter	6:30	8:30
4th Quarter	7:12	7:48
Third-Down Conversions	4 of 16	4 of 12
Fourth-Down Conversions	1 of 3	1 of 1
Red-Zone Scores-Chances	0-1	3-3
Touchdowns	0-1	3-3
Field Goals	0-1	0-3
Sacks By: Number-Yards	2-15	4-29
PAT Kicks	0-0	5-5
Field Goals	0-0	1-1
Points Off Turnovers	0	0

College Football Playoff Championship Game
Alabama 45 - Clemson 40

Jan. 11, 2016
Glendale, Arizona

	UA	CU
FIRST DOWNS	18	31
Rushing	6	9
Passing	11	20
Penalty	1	2
NET YARDS RUSHING	138	145
Rushing Attempts	46	38
Average Per Rush	3.0	3.8
Rushing Touchdowns	3	1
Yards Gained Rushing	179	175
Yards Lost Rushing	41	30
NET YARDS PASSING	335	405
Completions-Attempts-Int	16-25-0	30-47-1
Average Per Attempt	13.4	8.6
Average Per Completion	20.9	13.5
Passing Touchdowns	2	4

	UA	CU
TOTAL OFFENSE YARDS	473	550
Total Offense Plays	71	85
Average Gain Per Play	6.7	6.5
Fumbles: Number-Lost	0-0	2-0
Penalties: Number-Yards	2-21	4-27
PUNTS-YARDS	7-297	6-265
Average Yards Per Punt	42.4	44.2
Net Yards Per Punt	39.3	38.8
Inside 20	3	2
50+ Yards	1	2
Touchbacks	0	1
Fair Catch	5	0
KICKOFFS-YARDS	7-422	7-448
Average Yards Per Kickoff	60.3	64.0
Net Yards Per Kickoff	36.3	28.9
Touchbacks	4	2
Punt Returns: Number-Yards-TD	1-12-0	2-22-0
Average Per Return	12.0	11.0
Kickoff Returns: Number-Yds-TD	5-196-1	3-68-0
Average Per Return	39.2	22.7
Interceptions: Number-Yds-TD	1-0-0	0-0-0
Fumble Returns: Number-Yds-TD	0-0-0	0-0-0
Miscellaneous Yards	0	0
Possession Time	30:31	29:29
1st Quarter	7:57	7:03
2nd Quarter	9:35	5:25
3rd Quarter	5:24	9:36
4th Quarter	7:35	7:25
Third-Down Conversions	9 of 18	6 of 14
Fourth-Down Conversions	0 of 0	0 of 0
Red-Zone Scores-Chances	3-3	5-5
Touchdowns	2-3	3-5
Field Goals	1-3	2-5
Sacks By: Number-Yards	2-14	5-31
PAT Kicks	6-6	4-4
Field Goals	1-2	2-3
Points Off Turnovers	7	0

Nick Saban's College Head Coach Record

Nick Saban has won five national college football championships, including four at Alabama and one at LSU. He began his career as a head coach in 1990 at Toledo. Here is his year-by-year record as a college head coach:

YEAR	SCHOOL	RECORD	POSTSEASON BOWL OR FINISH
1990	Toledo	9-2	Mid-American Conference Co-Champions
1995	Michigan State	6-5-1	Independence Bowl
1996	Michigan State	6-6	Sun Bowl
1997	Michigan State	7-5	Aloha Bowl
1998	Michigan State	6-6	
1999	Michigan State	9-2	Citrus Bowl (Accepted LSU job before the game)
2000	LSU	8-4	Peach Bowl
2001	LSU	10-3	Sugar Bowl
2002	LSU	8-5	Cotton Bowl
2003	LSU	13-1	BCS National Champions; SEC Champions; Sugar Bowl
2004	LSU	9-3	Capital One Bowl
2007	Alabama	7-6 (2-6 after NCAA ruling)	Independence Bowl
2008	Alabama	12-2	Sugar Bowl
2009	Alabama	14-0	BCS National Champions; SEC Champions
2010	Alabama	10-3	Capital One Bowl
2011	Alabama	12-1	BCS National Champions
2012	Alabama	13-1	BCS National Champions; SEC Champions
2013	Alabama	11-2	Sugar Bowl
2014	Alabama	12-2	College Football Playoff; SEC Champions; Sugar Bowl
2015	Alabama	14-1	CFP National Champions; SEC Champions; Cotton Bowl

Sources: The Southeastern Conference, The National College Football Playoff, University of Alabama Athletics and CollegePressBox.com.

Author's Note and Acknowledgments

ALMOST NO HOUSEHOLD IN ALABAMA can claim neutrality when it comes to college football. You're either a Bama family, or you're for that school down there on the plains . . . Auburn.

In our house, it was all Crimson Tide. The first game I remember with any detail was Bama's January 1, 1965, Orange Bowl clash with Texas. My parents, brothers, and I watched the game at a family friend's house because they had a color television set. I didn't know it at the time, but this was the first Orange Bowl game played at night and helped usher in a new era of prime-time college football television broadcasts

And it lived up to expectations. An injured Joe Namath came off the bench and nearly led Alabama back to victory. But officials ruled that Namath fell short of the goal line on a quarterback sneak in the fourth quarter, and the Crimson Tide lost, 21-17. For me, an eight-year-old kid not yet completely obsessed with winning and losing, just seeing those crimson and white uniforms on national television was enough. There would be better days for Alabama football, and I would get a chance to be on hand to witness many of them.

On the field as Alabama's head coach that night in 1965 was the legendary Paul "Bear" Bryant. Many years later, as sports editor and then editor-in-chief of *The Crimson White*, the student newspaper at Alabama, I had a chance to interview Bryant on several occasions. My last interview with him came on a rare snowy day in Tuscaloosa in February 1979, not yet a year after I graduated. After the interview, as I prepared to leave his office in Memorial Coliseum (now Coleman Coliseum), he got his hat, put on a long coat, and said he would walk out with me. His wife, Mary Harmon Bryant, had been hospitalized briefly, and the coach was anxious to see her.

As we walked down the steps and out to the parking lot, the light snow continued to fall. He turned to me and said: "Son, you're a southerner, and I know you don't know how to drive in this stuff any better than I do. Be careful now." Despite his well-earned reputation for toughness, Bryant seemed all the world to me at that moment like a grandfather. In fact, he even looked like my own granddad that day, aging but tall in stature and authentic. There was nothing phony about coach Bryant, or my grandfather, Ernest Mayfield.

Less than four years later, on January 26, 1983, Bryant died of a heart attack. I was working for *USA Today* in the newspaper's Rosslyn, Virginia, headquarters when the news came. It was shocking. To me, and to thousands of others like me who grew up watching Alabama play football, it's not a stretch to say it felt like a close friend died.

It is simply impossible to overestimate Bryant's influence on Alabama, and the entire college football world. Bryant won six national championships at Alabama, and Gene Stallings and his

1992 team added another. But there was some tough sledding afterward as Alabama suffered severe NCAA sanctions, went through coach after coach, and simply could not recapture the magic that had been there before, even before Bryant, when legends like Frank Thomas and Wallace Wade had put the Crimson Tide on college football's map.

Then along came Nick Saban, a no-nonsense, proven winner who, actually, isn't about winning as much as he is about doing everything—from recruiting to workouts to classes to training to practice to every play—the right way. The winning is the result of it all. But in Nick Saban's world, the means are just as important as the ends.

I returned to Alabama from New York, and the chance to watch this program close up, in 2010, three years after Saban arrived on campus, and nearly a year after he led the Crimson Tide to a national title in 2009. Most of my career since leaving *USA Today* back in 1993 had been in the magazine business, with stops as editor-in-chief of *Traditional Home* and *House Beautiful* magazines, among others. But my attention had never strayed far from Alabama football. In 2012, I co-authored a book called *Crimson Domination* with Tommy Ford, assistant athletics director/donor programs at Alabama. That book focused on the Crimson Tide's 2012 national championship, won in dominating fashion with a 42-14 victory over Notre Dame in the Bowl Championship Series title game in Miami, Florida.

This new book, focused on the 2015 national championship, could not be possible, obviously, without the kind of success that Saban has brought to Tuscaloosa. For that I'm grateful, as are millions of Tide fans across the nation. Alabama, having now won four national championships in the past seven years, is in the midst of a truly historic run at college football's summit.

I have many people and organizations to thank for this book, and it would be impossible to mention all of them. But I must name a few, beginning with my family, which has indulged my passion for college football with patience, good humor, and love. Thanks to my four great children, Madison, Alexa, Matthew, and Stephanie. Matt and Steph are Bama grads, Maddie is a senior there now, and Alexa, entering the ninth grade this year, might someday make it four-for-four at Alabama. But I'll support her, of course, wherever she goes. Unless it's Auburn . . . just kidding!

Thanks also to my wife, Monica, who has stood by me all these years and offered more than a little advice as I poured through all the stats, transcripts, and interviews for this manuscript. She has always been my best editor.

I mentioned earlier that I grew up in a Bama family. But I have so much more to thank my parents for than mere football. Their guidance, steady advice, and support all these years have meant everything to me. As I say every chance I get: no one ever had better parents than Dewey and Phyllis Mayfield.

Thanks, as well, to all the students I have had the privilege of working with at the University of Alabama's Office of Student Media. The Crimson Tide wasn't the only national champion at Alabama in 2015. *The Crimson White*, the student newspaper, won the prestigious Associated Collegiate Press's Pacemaker Award as one of the best college publications in the nation. It has been a pleasure to serve as its adviser. And I must say thank you to Paul Wright, director of UA's Student Media office, who not only runs a great shop, but also is one of Alabama's most loyal fans. Paul and his wife, Susan, are regulars at nearly all UA sporting events, supporting teams with regular attendance, no matter the winning and losing. The very best kind of fans.

All the photos in the book's insert were taken by *The Crimson White*'s Layton Dudley, a superb young photographer who has a wonderful career ahead of her. Her excellent work speaks for itself.

Thanks are also due to *Crimson Magazine*, where I've covered the Tide's home games for most of these last few years, and specifically to owners Josh and Jim Watkins, and to previous owners Gregory Enns and Stephen Jackson.

Anyone who has ever sat in the press box at Bryant-Denny Stadium can attest to the expert way in which the Alabama Athletics Communication office goes about its work. There isn't a more professional group at any program in the country, and my thanks not only for the credentials these past few years, but also for the mountains of statistics, access to news conferences, and, I must mention: the food in the press box, too. Outstanding.

Thanks also to my three buddies in radio: George Brown, executive director of UA Recreation; Adam Sterritt, assistant vice president for UA Student Affairs; and Terry Siggers, general manager of WVUA-FM 90.7, The Capstone, our student radio station. George, Adam, and I fearlessly host a weekly show there called *Skybox*, on Saturday mornings during the football season. Terry often produces the show and has shown extreme patience in putting up with the three of us, who aren't exactly experienced radio hosts but are never shy about making our college football predictions. Every now and then we get one right.

And finally, and importantly, thanks to everyone at Skyhorse Publishing in New York, most especially to Niels Aaboe, executive editor, and Tony Lyons, president and publisher. It has been a pleasure to work with them, and I hope I have written a manuscript worthy of their commitment to publish it.

Resources

Alabama Athletics Communications Office/RollTide.com
The Southeastern Conference/SECSports.com
College Football Playoff
ESPN/ESPN.com/The SEC Network
The Paul Finebaum Show
USA Today
Alabama Media Group
The Tuscaloosa News
The Anniston Star
247Sports/BamaOnLine
The Montgomery Advertiser
The Times-Picayune/NOLA.com
The Crimson White
Crimson Magazine
WVUA-FM 90.7 The Capstone
WDGM-FM Radio Tide 99.1

Sports Illustrated
Yahoo Sports
CBS Sports
The Atlanta Journal-Constitution
The New York Times
Time Magazine
Forbes Magazine
GQ Magazine
The NFL Network
The Seattle Seahawks
The Indianapolis Colts
The Buffalo Bills
Spartan Sports Network
TigerNet.com
Gridiron Now
Burke, Monte, *Saban: The Making of a Coach* (Simon & Schuster, 2015)
Ford, Tommy and Mayfield, Mark, *Crimson Domination: The Process Behind Alabama's 15th National Championship* (Whitman Books, 2013)